My Samsung® Galaxy Tab™ 2

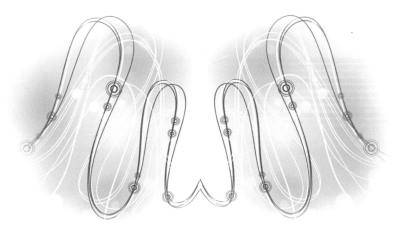

Eric Butow
Lonzell Watson

800 East 96th Street,
Indianapolis, Indiana 46240 USA

My Samsung® Galaxy Tab 2™

Copyright © 2013 by Pearson Education, Inc.

ISBN-13: 978-0-7897-5038-9

ISBN-10: 0-7897-5038-4

The Library of Congress cataloging-in-publication data is on file.

Printed in the United States of America

First Printing: December 2012

Trademarks

All terms mentioned in this book that are known to be trademarks or service marks have been appropriately capitalized. Que Publishing cannot attest to the accuracy of this information. Use of a term in this book should not be regarded as affecting the validity of any trademark or service mark.

All Galaxy Tab 2 images are provided by Samsung Electronics America.

Warning and Disclaimer

Every effort has been made to make this book as complete and as accurate as possible, but no warranty or fitness is implied. The information provided is on an "as is" basis. The author and the publisher shall have neither liability nor responsibility to any person or entity with respect to any loss or damages arising from the information contained in this book or from the use of programs accompanying it.

Bulk Sales

Que Publishing offers excellent discounts on this book when ordered in quantity for bulk purchases or special sales. For more information, please contact

U.S. Corporate and Government Sales
1-800-382-3419
corpsales@pearsontechgroup.com

For sales outside of the U.S., please contact

International Sales
international@pearsoned.com

Editor-in-Chief
Greg Wiegand

Acquisitions Editor
Michelle Newcomb

Development Editor
Charlotte Kughen

Managing Editor
Sandra Schroeder

Senior Project Editor
Anne Goebel

Indexer
Tim Wright

Proofreader
Kathy Ruiz

Technical Editor
Christian Kenyeres

Publishing Coordinator
Cindy Teeters

Book Designer
Anne Jones

Compositor
Mary Sudul

Contents at a Glance

Table of Contents

10   Capturing and Managing Photos   193

11   Using Maps, Navigation, Local, and Latitude   215

12   Enhancing Your Galaxy Tab 2 with Apps   241

13   Adding New Hardware   271

About the Authors

Eric Butow began writing books in 2000 when he wrote *Master Visually Windows 2000 Server*. Since then, Eric has authored or coauthored 19 other books. Those books include Addison-Wesley's *User Interface Design for Mere Mortals*, Amacom's *How to Succeed in Business Using LinkedIn*, Wiley Publishing's *Droid Companion*, Que Publishing's *My Samsung Galaxy Tab*, and, most recently, Que Publishing's *Blogging to Drive Business, Second Edition*.

Eric lives in Jackson, California. He has a Master's degree in communication from California State University, Fresno, and is the owner of Butow Communications Group (BCG), an online marketing ROI improvement firm.

Website: http://butow.net

LinkedIn: http://linkedin.com/in/ebutow

Lonzell Watson is the best-selling author of the *Teach Yourself Visually iPad* book series. His books have won the International Award of Excellence, the award of Distinguished Technical Communication and Best of Show presented by the Society for Technical Communication, for the past two years in a row. He is the author of other popular titles including *My Samsung Galaxy Tab, My HTC EVO 3D, Teach Yourself Visually Digital Video, Teach Yourself Visually Final Cut Pro*, and the *Canon VIXIA Digital Field Guide*.

Lonzell is an instructional designer in the aerospace and defense industry and is also an Adjunct Professor in the College of Business at Bellevue University. He holds a Master's degree in Instructional Design and Development and is the owner of Creative Intelligence LLC, an instructional design and technical writing company.

Website: http://creativeintel.com

LinkedIn: http://linkedin.com/pub/lonzell-watson/6/b64/499

Dedication

To all the daycare kids I helped take care of over the years. You're growing up in an exciting time.
—Eric Butow

To Antonio Tapia. Thank you so much for your guidance and insight. For this, I am forever grateful.
—Lonzell Watson

Acknowledgments

Eric Butow: My thanks as always to my family and friends. I want to thank my awesome literary agent, Carole Jelen, as well as Cindy Teeters, Greg Wiegand, and especially Michelle Newcomb. Finally, I want to thank my coauthor, Lonzell Watson, for his help making this book a reality.

Lonzell Watson: I would like to give special thanks to Michelle Newcomb, without whom this project would not have been possible. I would like to thank Antonio Tapia for all of his hard work and insight. Special thanks go to Laura Clor, to my lovely wife, Robyn, to Shannon Johnson, and Danya and Sean Platt.

We Want to Hear from You!

As the reader of this book, *you* are our most important critic and commentator. We value your opinion and want to know what we're doing right, what we could do better, what areas you'd like to see us publish in, and any other words of wisdom you're willing to pass our way.

As an editor-in-chief for Que Publishing, I welcome your comments. You can email or write me directly to let me know what you did or didn't like about this book—as well as what we can do to make our books better.

Please note that I cannot help you with technical problems related to the topic of this book. We do have a User Services group, however, where I will forward specific technical questions related to the book.

When you write, please be sure to include this book's title and author as well as your name, email address, and phone number. I will carefully review your comments and share them with the author and editors who worked on the book.

Email: feedback@quepublishing.com

Mail: Greg Wiegand
           Editor-in-Chief
           Que Publishing
           800 East 96th Street
           Indianapolis, IN 46240 USA

Reader Services

Visit our website and register this book at quepublishing.com/register for convenient access to any updates, downloads, or errata that might be available for this book.

Review the different
versions of Android

Meet the newest members
of the Galaxy Tab family: the Galaxy
Tab 2 7.0 and 10.1

Learn how the Galaxy Tab 2 compares
to other Galaxy Tab models

In this chapter, you're introduced to the different versions of Android and the different models of the Galaxy Tab including the Galaxy Tab 2. Topics in this chapter include:

→ The three different versions of the Android operating system

→ The two models of the Galaxy Tab 2

→ A comparison of Galaxy Tab 2 and other models in the Galaxy Tab family

The Galaxy Tab Universe

If you're brand new to the Galaxy Tab 2, start with this chapter so you can learn more about your new tablet and also learn more about the Android™ operating system that the Galaxy Tab 2 uses. If you want to get started right away, proceed to Chapter 2, "Meeting the Samsung Galaxy Tab 2."

First, a Look at Android

The Galaxy Tab 2 runs the Android operating system that is produced and maintained by Google. According to the latest IDC report as of this writing that tracked mobile operating system marketing share, in the first quarter of 2012 Android commanded 59 percent market share, well above the second place iOS used on iPhones and iPads (http://www.idc.com/getdoc. jsp?containerId=prUS23503312).

There are several versions of Android currently available that run on various smartphones and tablets. Each version is best known by the nicknames Google gives it. Since version 1.5, Google has given the name of a sweet treat to every new version; version 1.5 was known as Cupcake. (There were two previous versions before Cupcake that didn't have a nickname, so Google decided to give the third release of Android a nickname starting with the third letter of the alphabet.)

Galaxy Tab models run one of the following Android versions:

- Version 2.2, or Froyo (short for frozen yogurt), runs on the original Galaxy Tab 7.0. You can learn more about using Froyo on the Galaxy Tab 7.0 in our 2011 book *My Samsung Galaxy Tab* (ISBN 978-0-7897-4797-6).

- Version 2.3, Gingerbread, is the most widely used version of Android as of early July 2012 (http://developer.android.com/about/dashboards/ index.html). In addition to including user interface improvements, Gingerbread was designed for use on extra-large screen resolutions and provides improved network performance.

- Version 3, Honeycomb, was the first version optimized for use with tablets. It includes more user interface improvements, support for video chat using Google Talk, and the ability to encrypt all user data.

- Version 4, Ice Cream Sandwich, includes more improvements to the user interface, improved features, such as real time speech-to-text dictation, and new apps, such as a photo editor. The text and screenshots in this book are based on the latest version of Ice Cream Sandwich (as of this writing), Version 4.0.4.

You find out more about the versions each Galaxy Tab model uses later in this chapter.

What About Android 4.1, Jelly Bean?

As this book was being written in July 2012, Android released Version 4.1, or Jelly Bean, with improvements that include a new interface layout for tablets with smaller screens like the Galaxy Tab 2 7.0, an improved camera app, and the new Google Now personalized search app. Your Galaxy Tab 2 automatically checks for operating system updates so you receive those updates when they're available. You should also check the Android website often (http://www. android.com) to see about upcoming versions. By the time you read this another new version, rumored to be called Key Lime Pie, might be available.

The Newest Members: The Galaxy Tab 2 Family

Before we talk more about all the Galaxy Tab models Samsung offers, it's important to talk about the subject of this book and the two newest additions to the Galaxy Tab family: The Galaxy Tab 2. Both models run Ice Cream Sandwich and play the latest audio and video files, but there are several differences as well.

The Galaxy Tab 2 7.0

The Galaxy Tab 2 7.0 has a 7" screen, which explains how it got its name. The Tab 2 7.0 only comes with 8GB of RAM, but it does contain a microSD slot that can bring your total RAM to 32GB. The Tab 2 7.0 also includes

- Wi-Fi connectivity

- 1024 × 600 pixel screen resolution

- 3.0 megapixel rear camera

- 0.76 pound total weight

- Battery life of about 7 hours and 30 minutes (see http://www.engadget.com/2012/04/11/samsung-galaxy-tab-2-7-0-review/ for more information)

If you prefer to hold a tablet in one hand comfortably but you also want more screen space than a smartphone then consider the Tab 2 7.0. Unlike some of the e-readers out there (such as Amazon's Kindle), the Tab 2 7.0 comes with the full version of Ice Cream Sandwich as well as the Kindle app.

The Galaxy Tab 2 10.1

Soon after Samsung launched the Galaxy Tab 2 7.0, out came the Galaxy Tab 2 10.1. The Tab 2 10.1 is so named because of its 10.1" screen, which is one of the largest screens you can find on a tablet. The Tab 2 10.1 also includes

- Wi-Fi connectivity

- 16GB of RAM with a microSD slot that can bring the total RAM to 32GB

- Front camera with VGA (640 × 480 pixel) resolution for video calls

- 3.0 megapixel rear camera

- 1.28 pound total weight

- Battery life of nearly 9 hours (see http://www.engadget.com/2012/05/15/samsung-galaxy-tab-2-10-1-review/ for more information)

You can hold the Galaxy Tab 2 10.1 in one hand, but it's usually safer to hold it with both hands. If you want to have the most screen space available so you can use it for tasks that your laptop did (such as taking notes or watching movies) then the Tab 2 10.1 might be the right tablet for you.

If you want to learn more about each Tab 2 model and the differences between them, skip ahead to Chapter 2.

Comparing the Tab 2 to Other Tabs

There are now a total of seven different Galaxy Tabs, including the Tab 2 family. What's more, the Galaxy Note is a smartphone/tablet hybrid that we've included in this discussion.

Galaxy Tab 7.0

This is the original Galaxy Tab that Samsung produced. The Tab 7.0 was originally positioned as a smaller alternative to the iPad, which comes in only one size. Samsung decided that their Tab models would run various versions of Google's Android mobile operating system so the Tab would be compatible with other Android phones just as the iPad is compatible with the iPhone. The Tab 7.0 runs Froyo.

Though the Tab 7.0 Plus was designed to eventually replace the Tab 7.0, the original Tab 7.0 is still offered by AT&T, Sprint, Verizon, and T-Mobile. You can also buy a Wi-Fi only model. Prices vary between the carriers and the Wi-Fi version.

Galaxy Tab 7.0 Plus

The Tab 7.0 Plus is a sleeker version of the original Tab 7.0 that runs Honeycomb and has some more hardware and software features than the original Tab. Therefore, the Tab 7.0 Plus doesn't have the buttons below the screen like the original Tab 7.0 or the Galaxy Note. Instead, the Tab 7.0 Plus works like its larger siblings, the Tab 8.9 and Tab 10.1. The Tab 7.0 Plus is only offered by T-Mobile or as a Wi-Fi model. If you choose the Wi-Fi model, there are several different online vendors that sell it.

Galaxy Tab 7.7

The Tab 7.7 is not only a bit larger than the 7.0 models but it also boasts some interesting features. The screen is based on AMOLED technology with a 1200 × 800 pixel resolution. (AMOLED stands for active-matrix organic light emitting diode.) The Tab 7.7 includes a more powerful battery—5,100mAh compared to 4,000mAh on the 7.0 Plus—that results in longer usage times on a single charge. And unlike other Tab models, you can make and receive voice calls with the Tab 7.7.

Galaxy Tab 8.9

The Galaxy Tab 8.9 not only has a larger screen and a larger footprint, it also has a 1280 × 800 pixel screen. Like the 7.0 Plus, 7.7, and 10.1 models, the 8.9 runs Honeycomb. The Tab 8.9 is only offered by AT&T with 16GB of memory, although you can also buy a 16GB or 32GB Wi-Fi model from several vendors.

Galaxy Tab 10.1

If you're looking for the largest Tab model, or a larger Tab that's offered by more carriers, then you should consider the Tab 10.1. Like the Tab 8.9, the Tab 10.1 includes a screen that has 1280 × 800 pixel resolution and a screen size of 10.1". This screen is not only larger than the iPad 2 screen but also has greater resolution. The battery (7,000mAh) is the most powerful of any Tab and provides 9 hours of usage on a single charge.

Like the Tab 8.9, you can buy a Tab 10.1 with 16GB or 32GB of memory. The Tab 10.1 is offered by Verizon and T-Mobile but also comes in a Wi-Fi model as well. As of this writing, the Tab 10.1 was not being sold because of a patent dispute between Apple and Samsung.

Galaxy Note

In late 2011 and early 2012, Samsung released the 5.3" version of its Galaxy Note "phablet," which is a device that's larger than a phone but smaller than a tablet and has features of each. For example, the Note has buttons below the screen as the Tab 7.0 does because the Note runs Gingerbread. The Note comes with a stylus called an "S Pen" so you can manipulate screen elements, handwrite notes, and draw on apps created for use with the Note. Samsung is also developing a 10.1" version of the Note that will be released in the second half of 2012; the 10.1" Note will cost more than the Tab 10.1.

Choosing from all these models can be confusing, but you can't say that Samsung doesn't have an offering for nearly every potential tablet user. You can learn more about the Galaxy Tab and Note family and get updated information by visiting Samsung's website (http://www.samsung.com).

See the differences between the Galaxy Tab 2 7.0 and the Galaxy Tab 2 10.1

Take a tour of the physical buttons and switches on your Galaxy Tab 2

Familiarize yourself with what the four menu icons at the bottom of the
Galaxy Tab 2 screens do

View three important screens on your Galaxy Tab 2, including the home screen

Understand how to manipulate the screen

Learn how to interact with Android

In this chapter, you discover the different hardware and the common screens on both models of the Galaxy Tab 2. Topics covered in this chapter include:

→ Features on the front, back, and sides of the unit

→ Galaxy Tab 2 icons for manipulating the screen

→ Three important screens you need to know

→ How to manipulate the Galaxy Tab 2 screen

→ Configuring email settings

→ How to interact with Android

Meeting the Samsung Galaxy Tab 2

This book covers two models of the Galaxy Tab 2: the 7" Tab and the larger 10" version.

The 7" unit, called the Galaxy Tab 2 7.0, runs version 4.0 of Google's Android operating system, also called Ice Cream Sandwich.

The 10" unit, called the Galaxy Tab 2 10.1, also runs Ice Cream Sandwich. Both models connect to the Internet and/or a network using a Wi-Fi connection. (As of this writing no cell phone carrier has offered the Galaxy Tab 2 with its data network plans.)

Many tasks throughout the book include information for one model or the other, and if there are any differences between the two models then there are separate tasks for each. The headers for each section (or subsection) indicate in parentheses the model name, such as (Galaxy Tab 2 10"). If you don't see an area in parentheses in the section (or subsection) name, the information applies to both models.

Investigating the Galaxy Tab 2 Unit

Before you work with your Galaxy Tab 2, it's important to take it out of the box and examine it so you can learn where all the controls and features are on the unit. If you've used (or tried) another tablet computer in the past, you might already be familiar with some of the features. If this is your first time using a tablet computer or the Galaxy Tab 2, though, take time to read this chapter and enjoy learning about your new Tab 2.

Physical Features of the Galaxy Tab 2 7"

The front of the Galaxy Tab 2 7" includes the LCD touch screen for viewing information as well as a brightness sensor and a camera so you can take photos and/or record video of yourself.

You learn more about using the cameras to record video in Chapter 8, "Playing Music and Video," and to take photos in Chapter 10, "Capturing and Managing Photos."

Brightness sensor

Camera viewfinder

Touch screen

The back of the unit has only one feature: a second camera that includes a flash so you can take photos and record video using your Galaxy Tab 2. (Otherwise, the function of the back is to rest in your hand, of course.)

Camera

There are four buttons included on both the Galaxy Tab 2 7" and the Galaxy Tab 2 10". Those buttons are covered later in the chapter in the "The Galaxy Tab 2 Buttons and Switches" section. Aside from those four, the Galaxy Tab 2 7" contains a number of features on the sides of the unit:

- A microphone on the top side of the unit, which is useful for making phone calls and recording audio.

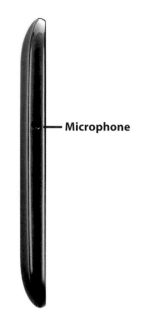

— **Microphone**

- A MicroSD memory card slot on the left side of the unit.

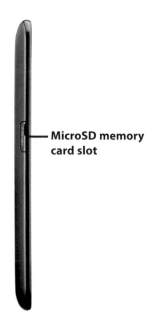

— **MicroSD memory card slot**

- The audio speakers on the bottom side of the unit.

- A dock/charge and sync cable connector that is also on the bottom side of the unit. You learn more about docking, charging, and syncing your Galaxy Tab 2 in Chapter 3, "Setting Up the Galaxy Tab 2."

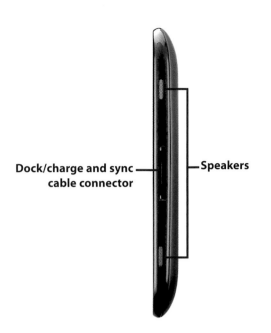

Dock/charge and sync —————| |—**Speakers**
cable connector

- The power button on the right side of the unit.

- The volume control slider also on the right side of the unit.

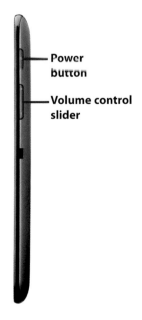

—**Power button**

—**Volume control slider**

Physical Features of the Galaxy Tab 2 10"

The front of the Galaxy Tab 2 10" includes the LCD touchscreen for viewing information and a camera so you can take photos or record video of yourself.

You learn more about using the cameras to record video in Chapter 8 and to take photos in Chapter 10.

Camera viewfinder

Touchscreen

The back of the unit has only one feature: a second camera that includes a flash so you can take photos and record video using your Galaxy Tab 2.

Camera

There are four buttons included on both the Galaxy Tab 2 7" and the Galaxy Tab 2 10". Those buttons are covered later in the chapter in the "The Galaxy Tab 2 Buttons and Switches" section. Aside from those four, the Galaxy Tab 2 10" contains a number of features on the sides of the unit.

- A headphone and microphone jack on the top side of the unit so you can either listen to audio privately or record audio into a microphone.

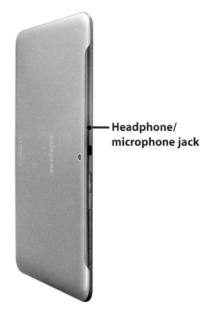

Headphone/ microphone jack

- The audio speakers on the left and right sides of the unit.

The speaker on the left side of the unit

- A dock/charge and sync cable connector that is on the bottom side of the unit. You learn more about docking, charging, and syncing your Galaxy Tab 2 in Chapter 3.

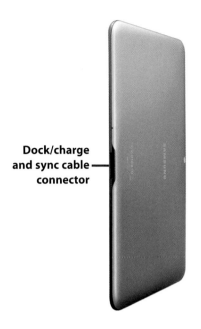

Dock/charge and sync cable connector

The Galaxy Tab 2 Buttons and Switches

Both models of the Galaxy Tab 2 feature four touch buttons at the bottom of the touch screen and a power button and volume slider on the right side of the unit.

Setting Up Your Galaxy Tab 2

When you start your Galaxy Tab 2 for the first time, you go through a series of steps to get your Tab 2 up and running including setting up your wireless connection. The four icons appear on your home screen after you set up the Tab 2. This book presumes that you have already set up your Tab 2 using the documentation that came in your Tab 2 box. If you need help with setting up a Wi-Fi network then you can find that information in Chapter 3.

The Four Galaxy Tab 2 Icons

There are four icons in the black Notification bar at the bottom of the screen that you use frequently to manage the device and applications on it. They are (from left to right) Back, Home, Task Manager, and Screen Shot.

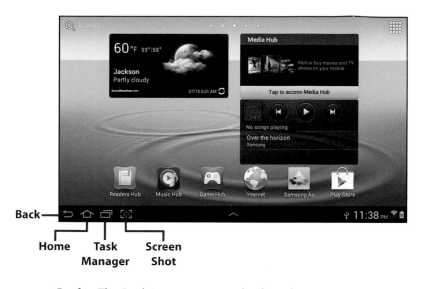

Back

Home   Task   Screen
       Manager   Shot

- **Back**—The Back icon moves you back to the previous screen. For example, if you're on the Home screen and touch the current time at the bottom right of the screen to bring up the Settings area, you might decide that you don't want to change settings. Close the settings area at the bottom of the screen by tapping the Back icon.

- **Home**—The Home icon is the most important icon because it's the icon you touch to get out of a specific application, such as the Galaxy Tab 2 web browser, and move back to the Home screen so you can open another application.

  If you want to hide an application and go back to the Home screen, tapping the Home icon is the way to go. Tapping the Home icon hides the application you currently have open.

- **Task Manager**—The Task Manager icon opens the Task Manager area on the left side of the screen so you can see what apps are open currently. Open the app on the screen by tapping the app thumbnail screen in the Task Manager app list.

Task Manager area

How Do I Close an App in Task Manager?

When you open an app and move to another task, that app stays open in the background. If you want to close an app in the Task Manager list, hold your finger down on the app thumbnail screen until a pop-up menu appears next to the thumbnail screen. Close the app by tapping Remove from List in the menu.

- **Screen Shot**—The Screen Shot icon makes it easy for you to take a picture of what's currently on the Galaxy Tab 2 screen so you can send it to someone. (It's also handy when taking screen shots for a book.) Just tap the Screen Shot icon to take the shot. After the Tab 2 takes the shot it opens the screen shot editor app and displays the shot you just took so you can make changes to it (such as trimming the screen shot using the Crop tool), save it, or discard it.

**The screen shot of the
Home screen in the
screen shot editor**

The Power Button

The Power button performs a number of important functions on your Galaxy Tab 2:

- Turns on the unit when you press the button. The Power button is on the right side of the Galaxy Tab 2 7" unit and on the top of the Galaxy Tab 2 10" unit. The Galaxy Tab 2 boots up and is ready for you to use in about 20 seconds.

- Turns off the unit when you press the button for about 10 seconds.

- If you press and hold the button for a few seconds while the unit is on, the Galaxy Tab 2 automatically goes into sleep mode and locks the device.

- When the unit is in sleep mode, press the Power button and hold it for a few seconds to wake up the Galaxy Tab 2.

Power button on the Galaxy Tab 2 7"

Power button on the Galaxy Tab 2 10"

What Happens if I Don't Turn Off the Galaxy Tab 2?

If the Galaxy Tab 2 is idle for a long period of time, the unit goes into sleep mode automatically. Sleep mode drains very little battery power, so if the Galaxy Tab 2 is frequently in sleep mode, you don't need to recharge your battery as often. Refer to Chapter 15, "Troubleshooting Your Galaxy Tab 2," for information about expected battery life and strategies for extending that lifespan.

Volume Control Buttons

There are two volume control buttons on the left side of the device—one that turns up the volume and one that turns down the volume. What device the buttons control depends on what you have connected to the Galaxy Tab 2.

Volume control buttons on the Galaxy Tab 2 7"

Volume control buttons on the Galaxy Tab 2 10"

If you're listening to audio through the Galaxy Tab 2 speakers, the unit remembers the volume settings for the external speakers and sets the volume accordingly. If you decide to connect headphones to the unit, the Galaxy Tab 2 adjusts to the headphone volume the unit has in memory. When you remove the headphones, the unit readjusts the volume to the speaker volume.

You might want to check your volume settings for your headphones and external speakers so you don't get any nasty surprises. You learn more about setting the volume in Chapter 3.

Galaxy Tab 2 Screens

There are three important screens that are mainstays of your Galaxy Tab 2 experience no matter which Galaxy Tab 2 model you use.

The Lock Screen (Galaxy Tab 2 7")

The lock screen is the default state of the Galaxy Tab 2 when it first boots.

The lock screen shows the current date and time as well as the Wi-Fi connectivity status and battery charge status in the lower-right corner of the screen.

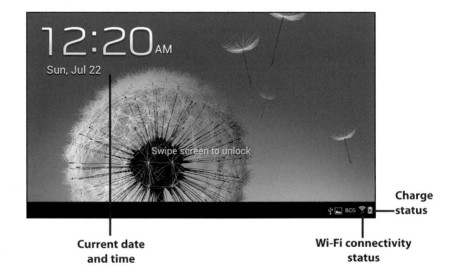

Charge status

Current date and time

Wi-Fi connectivity status

All you have to do to unlock your Tab 2 is to hold your finger anywhere on the screen and then swipe your finger in any direction. If your Tab 2 is password-protected then you need to type your password in the password box. You learn more about password-protecting your Galaxy Tab 2 in Chapter 3.

The Lock Screen (Galaxy Tab 2 10")

The lock screen is the default state of the Galaxy Tab 2 when it first boots.

The lock screen shows the current date and time, the current status of your Bluetooth and Internet connections, the amount of charge you have in your battery, and the Lock icon if you don't have a password. The black Notification bar at the bottom of the screen keeps you apprised of what's happening with your Galaxy Tab 2 at a glance. You can slide the Lock icon in any direction to open the applications screen.

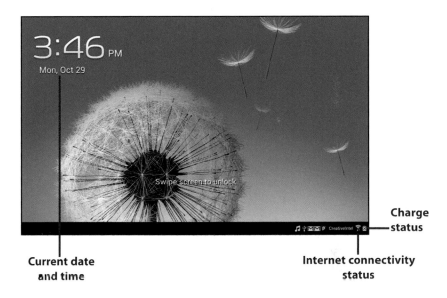

Charge status

Current date and time

Internet connectivity status

If your Galaxy Tab 2 is password-protected, the password box appears on the screen. You must tap the password box, type your password, and then tap the OK button to open the Home screen or the application you were working on before you put the unit to sleep. You learn more about password protecting your Galaxy Tab in Chapter 3.

The Apps Screen (Galaxy Tab 2 7")

The applications screen is your command center where you can access all the applications available on the Galaxy Tab 2. Tap the Applications icon at the upper-right corner of the Home screen to view the applications screen.

The Applications icon on the Home screen

When you tap an application icon, the application launches. If you have more than one page of application icons on the applications screen, dots appear at the bottom of the screen. You can scroll between pages by clicking one of the buttons or dragging or flicking left and right. You learn more about dragging and flicking later in this chapter.

Two buttons on the bottom of the screen

The Application Screen (Galaxy Tab 2 7")

After you press an application button on the applications screen, the application launches and takes up the entire screen. For example, if you open the Gmail application, a list of your incoming email appears on the screen.

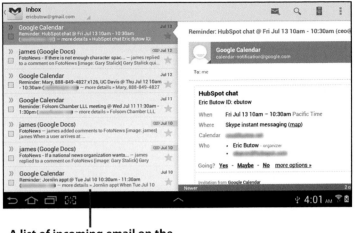

**A list of incoming email on the
Gmail application screen**

Manipulating the Screen

Like many tablets these days, the Galaxy Tab 2 doesn't come with a stylus
(essentially a stick) for manipulating elements on the screen. Instead, you use
your fingers and change the orientation of the Galaxy Tab 2 itself to make it
do what you want. Although the examples in this section are for the Galaxy
Tab 2 7", you manipulate elements on the Galaxy Tab 2 10" screen in the same
way. If there are different instructions for manipulating the screen for the Tab
10" model, we note them in a different subsection.

Tapping an Element

Unlike a desktop or laptop computer, you don't have a mouse installed on
your Galaxy Tab 2, so there is no cursor that you can see. However, when you
quickly tap an element with your finger, the Galaxy Tab 2 performs an action.
For example, when you tap an application icon, the Galaxy Tab 2 launches the
application.

You can also double-tap, which is two quick taps in the same location, to perform a specific function. For example, you can double-tap an image to zoom
in and double-tap again to zoom out.

Pinching

Apple set the standard for multitouch screen gesture requirements with its iPad, and the Galaxy Tab 2 follows the same standard. A multitouch screen can recognize different gestures that use multiple finger touches. One such gesture is the pinching gesture.

You pinch when you touch the screen with both your thumb and forefinger and bring them together in a pinching motion. This is also called pinching in, and it has the same effect as zooming in. For example, you can get a closer view of a web page in the browser by pinching. You can also pinch outward, which has the same effect as zooming out, by touching the screen with your thumb and forefinger together and moving them apart.

Dragging and Flicking

You can drag up and down the screen (or even left to right if an app allows it) by touching the top of the screen and moving your finger to drag content the length of the screen. If you want to move more content down the screen, remove your finger, touch the top of the screen, and drag your finger down the length of the screen again. You can drag a page of content up by touching the bottom of the screen and dragging your finger upward.

Dragging can become cumbersome, though, if you have to drag through a long document such as a web page or spreadsheet. The Galaxy Tab 2 makes it easy for you to drag through large chunks of content by flicking. That is, after you touch the top (or bottom) of the screen, move your finger quickly down (or up) and then lift your finger at the last moment so the content scrolls after you lift your finger. You can wait for the content to stop scrolling when you reach the beginning or end of the content, or you can touch anywhere on the screen to stop scrolling.

Screen Rotation and Orientation

Your Galaxy Tab 2 has two screen orientation modes—vertical and horizontal—and it knows which way it's oriented. By default, the Galaxy Tab 2 screen orientation changes when you rotate the unit 90 degrees so the screen is horizontal, or you can rotate it another 90 degrees so the screen is vertical again. Nearly all default apps, such as the Browser, use both orientations. However, there might be times when you don't want the Galaxy Tab 2 to automatically change its screen orientation when you move the unit. For example, you might want to view a web page only in vertical orientation.

You can set the autorotation setting on or off as you see fit.

1. Tap the clock at the far right of the Notification bar (in the lower-right corner of the screen).

2. Tap the Screen rotation button. The bar at the bottom of the button turns gray to signify that orientation lock is on.

3. Tap the Screen rotation button again to turn off orientation lock. The next time you rotate the unit 90 degrees, the screen rotates automatically.

Tap the clock in the Notification bar

The gray Screen rotation button indicates orientation lock is on

Interacting with Android

Android is a fun operating system to use; it includes a number of common elements, including sliders and switches, as well as the keyboard that you can use to enter and edit text in your Galaxy Tab 2.

Sliders

A slider is a button that requires a bit more effort for you to activate. Android uses sliders to prevent you from doing something that can lead to unintended consequences. For example, if you tap the clock in the Notification bar to open the status box, you see the Brightness slider so you can adjust the brightness of the screen.

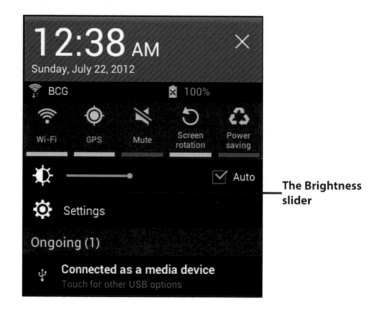

The Brightness slider

Settings Menus

You might see Settings menu icons at the top right of specific screens that provide more controls over a specific function. The Settings menu icon, a series of three vertical boxes, might disappear, or the menu functions might be different depending on the type of app you have open. For example, when you tap the Search icon on the Home screen, tap the Settings menu icon to open the Search settings menu and change your search options.

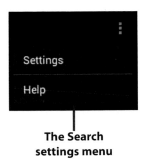

**The Search
settings menu**

Button Bar

You might see a button bar in different locations on the screen depending on the app you're using. For example, if you read an email message, you see a list of buttons in the bar at the top of the screen so you can perform certain tasks, such as replying to the message.

**A button bar at the top
of an email message**

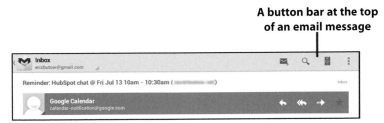

Tab Areas

Some apps have a Tab area at a location on the screen that contains a set of buttons that control the app. The area location and buttons vary depending on the app; if the app doesn't have a Tab area, you won't see one. For example, if you tap the Downloads app you see a Tab area in the center of the screen that enables you to view Internet downloads or any other type of download.

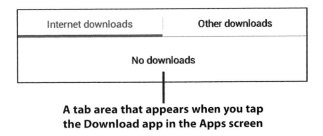

**A tab area that appears when you tap
the Download app in the Apps screen**

Using the Keyboard

The Galaxy Tab 2 doesn't come with a physical keyboard like you find on many smartphones. Instead, you type in the text with something that looks similar to a computer keyboard. The keyboard appears at the bottom of the screen automatically when you want to enter text.

The keyboard

You can type the letter by tapping the letter key. For example, if you tap the letter *a* on the keyboard, the lowercase letter *a* appears on the screen.

A lowercase a

>>>Go Further

HOW DO I CAPITALIZE A LETTER?

There are two ways you can capitalize a letter:

- Tap the Shift key and then tap the letter you want to capitalize. Notice that after you tap the Shift key that all the keys on the keyboard become capitalized.

The Shift key

- You can capitalize more than one letter by tapping the Shift key twice. The Shift key turns blue; this denotes that the Shift key is locked. You can unlock the Shift key by tapping the key again. You know the Shift key is unlocked not only because the white light on the Shift key is off, but also because all the letter keys on the keyboard are back to lowercase.

Using Special Keyboards and Characters

It's not easy typing on a screen that's only 7" wide (or even 10"), especially with an onscreen keyboard, but Android has a trick to make it a bit easier to add information.

The standard Tab keyboard doesn't include any numbers and not very many punctuation marks, but you can access more keys by tapping the ?123 key to see all 10 digits and a number of symbols.

The ?123 key

You can access an extended symbols keyboard by tapping the 1/2 key on the numbers and symbols keyboard. After you tap this key, the key label changes to 2/2. This signifies that you are on the second of two extended keyboards. When you're on the second extended keyboard, you can return to the numbers and symbols keyboard by tapping the 2/2 key.

The 1/2 key

My Keyboard Doesn't Look the Same!

Your keyboard options might change somewhat depending on the app you're in. For example, if you're typing an email message in the Gmail app, you see the @ key to the left of the spacebar because that's a key that you use often when typing an email address.

If you hold down a key on the keyboard, the letter appears, and if there are any related letters, such as a letter with an umlaut (such as ü), you see a button list above the board that lets you add the special character. If you don't want to add the special character, click the X button to close the button list.

A button list of special characters

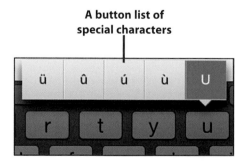

What Does the Clipboard Key Do?

To the right of the spacebar you see a key that has a clipboard on it. When you tap on the key the Clipboard area appears and shows you the eight most recent text and images you have in the Clipboard. Each text snippet and image appears in its own box. Edit or delete the snippet by tapping the Edit button or save the snippet to a file by tapping the Save button. When you're finished, tap the down arrow button to close the Clipboard area and return to the keyboard.

Copying and Pasting Data

Android makes it pretty easy to copy and paste text from one app to another. In this example, you learn to copy a term from the Browser app and paste it into the Search app so you can search for the term not only on the Web but also throughout the Galaxy Tab 2.

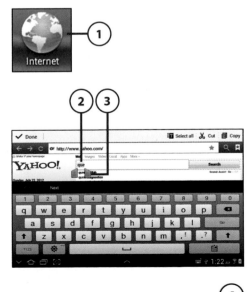

1. Launch the Internet app.

2. For this example, we start on the Yahoo! website. Type a search term into the Yahoo! search box.

3. Hold down your finger on the search box for a couple of seconds and then release your finger. The search term is highlighted and bracket bars appear below and on each side of the term.

4. In the Edit Text menu, tap Copy.

5. Tap the Search button.

6. Hold down your finger on the Google box until the Edit Text menu appears above the Search or Enter URL box and then release your finger.

7. In the Edit Text menu, tap Paste to insert the copied text.

Learn how to get details about the
Galaxy Tab 2

Learn how to set up your network

Learn about synchronizing the
Galaxy Tab 2 with other computers

In this chapter, you discover more about your Galaxy Tab 2 and how to connect it with other computers and networks, including:

→ Getting details about the Galaxy Tab 2

→ Setting up your network

→ Syncing the Galaxy Tab 2

Setting Up the Galaxy Tab 2

You can easily find information about the Galaxy Tab 2 so you can make changes as needed. When you finish making general changes to the Galaxy Tab 2, it's time to set up the network so your Galaxy Tab 2 can connect with the Internet. Finally, you learn how to synchronize your Galaxy Tab 2 with other devices, such as your desktop or laptop PC.

Getting Details About the Galaxy Tab 2

If you want to get information about the features in your Galaxy Tab 2 from one place, you can do so in the About section of the Settings app.

1. Tap the Clock in the Notification bar.

2. Tap Settings.

3. Scroll down the list and then tap About Device.

4. See the model number for your Galaxy Tab 2.

5. See the Android and Kernel versions.

6. Scroll down to see the build number for your Galaxy Tab 2.

7. Scroll back up and tap Status.

8. View the status of your Galaxy Tab 2, including battery status and charge level, phone number, signal strength, your Wi-Fi MAC address, and the current uptime (that is, how long your Galaxy Tab 2 has been on continuously). You need to scroll down to see the Wi-Fi MAC address, Bluetooth address, and uptime.

9. Tap the Back icon.

10. Tap Legal Information to view legal information about your Galaxy Tab 2.

About device

Software update

⑦— Status
Show status of battery, network, and other information

Legal information

④— Model number
GT-P3113

⑤— Android version
4.0.4

Kernel version
3.0.8-814538-user
se.infra@SEI-45 #1
SMP PREEMPT Tue Jul 3 22:12:32 KST 2012

Status

Battery status
Discharging

Battery level
100%

⑧— IP address
192.168.137.210

Wi-Fi MAC address
28:98:7B:DE:C3:E3

Bluetooth address
28:98:7B:DE:C3:E2

Serial number

⑩— Legal information

Model number
GT-P3113

>>>Go Further

MORE ABOUT THE STATUS BAR

The Status bar is the black bar at the bottom of your screen. The bar contains the four Galaxy Tab icons at the left side of the bar that we talked about in Chapter 2, "Meeting the Samsung Galaxy Tab 2." An up arrow appears in the middle of the bar, and when you tap the arrow you see six apps that you might use often: Alarm, Calculator, Email, Music Player, S Planner (that is, the built-in calendar on the Galaxy Tab 2), and the Task Manager. You find out how to open the apps from the Status bar as you go through the book. On the right side of the bar you see the system clock and icons that indicate your Wi-Fi connectivity and battery charge status. You might also see icons to the left of the clock, such as a USB icon (as shown in the figure) if you have the USB cable connected between your Tab 2 and your computer.

Setting Up Your Network

Now that you're familiar with the details about your Galaxy Tab 2 and accessing the Settings app, you need to use the Settings app to do one very important setup task: connect your Galaxy Tab 2 to the Internet. Depending on the phone carrier you use, you can connect with the Internet through a Wi-Fi connection. You also can connect to other devices and networks using a Bluetooth connection or through a VPN.

I Don't Have a Wireless Network...What Do I Do?

If you don't have a Wi-Fi network but you do have a high-speed Internet connection through a telephone (DSL) or cable (broadband) provider, you have several options. First, call your provider and ask for a new network modem that enables wireless connections. Second, ask how much the modem costs—some providers might give you a free upgrade.

Another option is to keep your current box and add a wireless base station of your own, such as ones offered by Apple and Microsoft.

Setting Up Wi-Fi

1. On the Home screen, tap the clock in the Notification bar.

2. Tap Settings.

3. Tap Wi-Fi if Wi-Fi is not selected already.

4. Tap Add Network in the Settings bar.

5. Type the network SSID into the Network SSID field.

6. Tap the Security field to set the security level.

7. Select the security level; the default is None.

8. Tap Save.

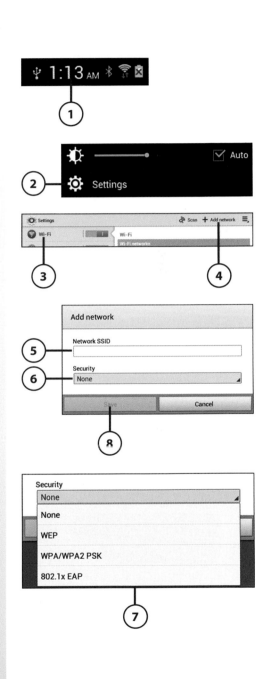

It's Not All Good

BE SECURE FIRST!

Your wireless network equipment should have security enabled. You know that security is enabled on the Wi-Fi network when you view the Wi-Fi Settings screen and see a padlock next to the Wi-Fi network in the list. When you select the Wi-Fi network for the first time, you should be asked to supply a password.

If you don't require a password, strongly consider adding one because unsecured networks send unencrypted (plain text) data—such as passwords and credit card numbers—through the air. Anyone else who has a Wi-Fi connection can tap in to your unsecured network and see what you're doing online. If you need more information, consult your network equipment documentation and/or manufacturer's website.

>>>Go Further

DISABLE WIRELESS CONNECTIONS ON A PLANE

When you're flying, the flight attendants always remind you to turn off your wireless devices during takeoffs and landings. You can quickly disable your wireless connections until you get to a safe flying altitude and the pilot gives you permission to turn on wireless devices again. Here's how:

1. Tap the clock in the Notification bar.

2. Tap Settings.

3. Tap More Settings.

4. Tap Airplane Mode.

The check box turns green to inform you that wireless connections are disabled. Tap Airplane Mode again to enable wireless connections.

Setting Up Bluetooth

1. Tap the clock in the Notification bar.

2. Tap Settings.

3. Tap the Bluetooth slider to turn on Bluetooth.

4. Tap the check box to the right of the device name if you want your Galaxy Tab 2 to be discovered by other computers and/or devices that you can connect to using a Bluetooth connection.

5. Tap Scan in the Settings toolbar.

6. Tap on a found device to connect with that device. You can rescan for devices by tapping Scan.

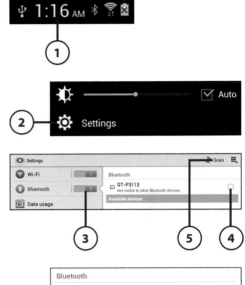

Setting Up a VPN

A VPN lets users in a public network (such as the Internet) transfer private data by making it appear to the users that they're in a private network of their own. For example, you can set up a VPN between yourself and your boss at the office so you can send private company data securely.

1. Tap the clock in the Notification bar.

2. Tap Settings.

3. Tap More Settings.

4. Tap VPN.

5. Tap Add VPN Network.

6. In the Edit VPN Network window, enter the VPN information including the VPN name and server address.

7. When you're finished, tap Save.

8. Tap the VPN name in the list.

9. Type the VPN username in the User Name field and the password in the Password field.

10. When you're done, tap Connect.

How to Disconnect from Your VPN

You can disconnect from the VPN by opening the Notifications panel at the top of the screen, tapping the VPN notification name, and then tapping Disconnect. It's as simple as that.

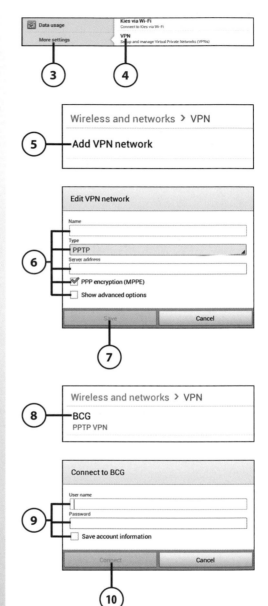

Syncing the Galaxy Tab 2

Synchronizing your Galaxy Tab 2 with your desktop or laptop computer has a number of advantages.

The Galaxy Tab 2 stores a backup of its contents on your desktop or laptop every time you sync both devices, so if you lose your data on the Galaxy Tab 2—or lose the Galaxy Tab 2 itself—you can restore the data from the backed up copies on your computer. What's more, if you have music, photos, or video on your computer, you can choose and copy a selection of those files onto your Galaxy Tab 2.

Android prefers Windows when it comes to syncing, and that's no surprise considering that Windows is the leading operating system for desktop PCs by far. This chapter describes how to sync music with the Galaxy Tab 2 in Windows. Later chapters cover how to sync other types of data, such as contacts.

Can I Sync Between the Galaxy Tab 2 and the Mac OS?

Syncing music from iTunes on the Mac OS to the Galaxy Tab 2 requires that you download additional software for your Mac. JRTStudio (www.jrtstudio.com) produces iSyncr, a utility that syncs what you have in iTunes with Android devices. As of this writing, the main app costs $2.99 in the Google Play Store, and that app enables you to sync your Tab 2 with iTunes on your Mac by connecting your Tab 2 to your Mac using the Tab 2 cable. You can purchase the Wi-Fi add-on app for 99 cents to sync your Mac and Tab 2 wirelessly.

It's easy to sync music files in Windows Media Player, the default music and multimedia player in Windows, to your Galaxy Tab 2 7".

1. Connect the Galaxy Tab 2 to your computer with the USB cable that came with your Galaxy Tab 2 if you haven't done so already.

2. Tap the clock in the Notification bar.

3. Tap Settings.

4. Tap Accounts and Sync.

5. By default your applications sync automatically at any time. If you don't want applications to sync data automatically, slide the Auto-sync slider to the left. (The slider button turns from green with an I to gray with an O).

6. Tap Add Account to add an account to sync.

7. Tap the type of account you want to add: an integrated social networking account, a corporate account, or a Google account. The next steps you see are determined by the type of account you add; for example, if you add a Facebook account then you're asked to log into your Facebook account so you can install the sync app for Facebook. When you finish setting up the account, your account appears in the Manage Accounts list.

8. Sync all accounts immediately by tapping Sync All. The Galaxy Tab 2 syncs all your accounts automatically; note that you don't need to enter your username and password for each account.

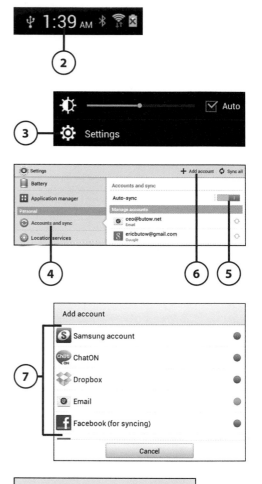

>>>Go Further

SYNC WITH ITUNES

It's also easy to sync your Galaxy Tab 2 with iTunes. You can mount the USB drive on the Galaxy Tab 2; then, on your computer, you can drag songs from iTunes and drop them to that drive. You can also sync to iTunes wirelessly by downloading the TuneSync app from the Android Market or from Highwind Software (www.highwindsoftware.com) for only $5.99. Highwind also makes a free Lite version if you want to check it out first, but this version limits playlists to 20 songs.

Learn how to password-protect your Galaxy Tab 2

Learn how to set parental restrictions

Learn about modifying screen wallpaper

Learn about setting alert sounds

Learn how to change keyboard settings

Your Galaxy Tab 2 isn't just a static system that forces you to work with it. It's malleable so you can change many attributes of the system to work the way you prefer. The topics in this chapter include the following:

→ Password-protecting the Galaxy Tab 2
→ Setting parental restrictions
→ Changing the date and time
→ Modifying your wallpaper
→ Setting alert sounds
→ Changing keyboard settings

Customizing Android 4

Password-Protecting the Galaxy Tab 2

One of the first things you should do when you set up your Galaxy Tab 2 is password-protect it so that unauthorized persons can't use your Galaxy Tab 2 or gain access to the data stored on it.

1. Tap the clock in the Notification bar.

2. Tap Settings.

3. Tap Security.

4. Tap Screen Lock.

5. Tap Password.

6. Type your password in the Select Password screen. The password must be at least four characters. A couple of seconds after you tap the letter, the letter turns into a dot to hide what you just entered. Tap Continue.

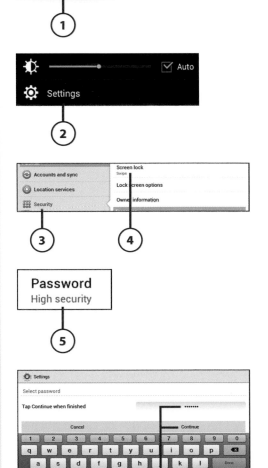

7. Retype the password in the Confirm Password screen (which is identical to the Select Password screen) and then tap OK.

The next time you log in to your Galaxy Tab 2, you are prompted to type in your password in the password box. If the keyboard doesn't appear on the screen right away, tap the password box to open the keyboard.

Select password	
Confirm password	•••••••
Cancel	OK

⑦

12:20 AM
Sat, July 28

Type your password in the password box

WHAT IF I CAN'T REMEMBER MY PASSWORD?

>>>Go Further

If you can't remember your password, your only recourse is to reset your Galaxy Tab 2 so that you wipe all the data from it and start from scratch. Unfortunately, this means that all your other data is wiped off the unit as well. Use the following steps to reset your Tab.

1. Turn your Galaxy Tab 2 off if it isn't already. You might need to remove the battery to turn off the unit.

2. Press and hold the Power and Volume Up buttons.

3. When you see the Samsung Galaxy Tab 2 logo, release the Power button but continue to hold the Volume Up button.

4. When the recovery screen appears, tap the Volume Down button until wipe data/factory reset is highlighted.

5. Press the Power button.

6. In the next screen, press the Volume Down button until Yes—Delete All User Data is highlighted.

7. Press the Power button.

8. After the Galaxy Tab 2 wipes the system data, press the Power button to reboot the system.

Changing Your Password

It's a good idea to change your password regularly so you have the peace of mind of knowing that you're keeping one step ahead of potential thieves.

1. Tap the clock in the Notification bar.

2. Tap Settings.

3. Tap Security.

4. Tap Screen Lock.

5. Type your password in the Confirm Password screen and then tap Continue.

6. Tap Password.

7. Type your password in the Select Password screen. The password must be at least four characters. A couple of seconds after you tap the letter, the letter turns into a dot to hide what you just entered. Tap Continue.

Select password

Tap Continue when finished   ········

Cancel   Continue

⑦

8. Retype the password in the Confirm Password screen (which is identical to the Select Password screen) and then tap OK. The next time you log in to your Galaxy Tab 2 you are prompted to type in your new password.

Select password

Confirm password   ········

Cancel   OK

⑧

>>>Go Further

ENTER A PATTERN OR NUMERIC PIN

The Galaxy Tab 2 gives you one of three options for password-protecting your unit: a text password, a numeric PIN (such as the one you use for an ATM card), or a pattern that you can draw on the screen. In the Screen Unlock Settings screen, tap Pattern or PIN to create a new pattern or numeric PIN, respectively. Then follow the step-by-step instructions to set the PIN.

Setting Parental Restrictions

Android 4 doesn't include parental restriction settings for specific applications aside from the pattern, PIN, or text password used for full access to the Galaxy Tab 2.

However, you can find parental control apps in the Google Play Store. Search for "parental control" or "parental controls," read the user reviews for each app, and then decide whether you want to download an app to see if it works for you.

An example of a parental control app in the Google Play Store

Change Your Content Filter Settings in the Google Play Store

You can determine what types of apps are shown to anyone who uses your Galaxy Tab 2 by setting the content filtering settings within the Google Play Store. You can show all apps or you can show apps by maturity level. You find out more about how to do this in Chapter 12, "Enhancing Your Galaxy Tab 2 with Apps."

Changing the Date and Time

You can set the date and time for your Galaxy Tab 2, change the time zone, change the date format, and display whether you want to display the time as standard 12-hour or 24-hour (military) time.

1. Tap the clock in the Notification bar.

2. Tap Settings.

3. Tap Date and Time.

4. Tap Set Date.

5. Tap the month, date, or year to change the date information. You can also tap the up and down arrow buttons above and below the month, date, or year to move the information up or down one month, one date, or one year, respectively.

6. Tap Set.

7. Tap Select Time Zone.

8. Tap the time zone for your locality.

9. Tap Set Time.

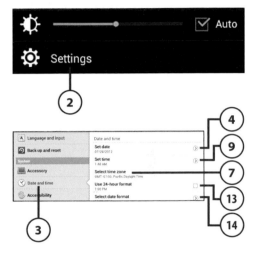

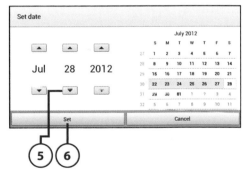

10. Tap the hour and/or minute to change the time information. You can also tap the up or down arrow buttons above and below the hour or minute to move the hour or minute by one hour or one minute, respectively.

11. Tap the AM or PM button to change the time of day between AM and PM.

12. Tap Set.

13. Tap Use 24-hour Format to change the format to 24-hour time. Note that the time on the Notification bar reflects the change. You can return to 12-hour time by tapping Use 24-hour Format again.

14. Tap Select Date Format.

15. Change the date format by tapping one of the three format options. If you don't want to change the date format, tap Cancel.

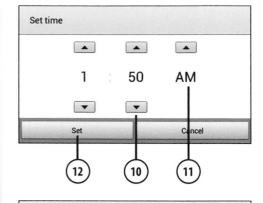

Modifying Your Wallpaper

The standard wallpaper appears behind both the lock screen and the Home screen. Android makes it easy for you to change the wallpaper to whatever you want.

1. Tap the clock in the Notification bar.

2. Tap Settings.

3. Tap Wallpaper.

4. Tap Home Screen, Lock Screen, or Home and Lock Screens depending on where you want to display your wallpaper. This example uses the Home and Lock Screens option.

5. Select where you want to get the wallpaper by tapping Gallery, Live Wallpapers, or Wallpapers.

6. Scroll through the thumbnail images of wallpapers.

7. When you find wallpaper you want, tap Set Wallpaper. The new wallpaper appears on your Home and lock screens.

The Difference Between Wallpaper and Live Wallpaper

So what makes wallpaper "live" on the Galaxy Tab 2? The difference is animation. For example, if you select the Bubbles live wallpaper then you see the bubbles move around and fade in and out in the background screen. Regular wallpaper doesn't have any animated features.

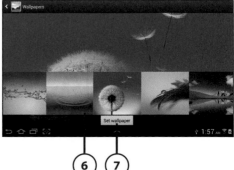

Setting Alert Sounds

If you want the Galaxy Tab 2 to make noise when you perform different actions, such as when you tap something on the screen, you can change the alert sounds or turn them off entirely.

1. Tap the clock in the Notification bar.

2. Tap Settings.

3. Tap Sound.

The One Guaranteed Solution for Silence

The Galaxy Tab 2 makes certain noises by default. For example, the unit plays tones when you use the dial pad on the phone.

If you really want to ensure that the unit doesn't make any noise, the one foolproof solution is to turn off the Galaxy Tab 2 unit.

4. Tap Volume.

5. Change the volume for music, video, games, and other media, notifications, and system sounds by dragging the appropriate slider bar to the left (lower volume) or right (higher volume).

6. Tap OK.

7. Tap Default Notifications.

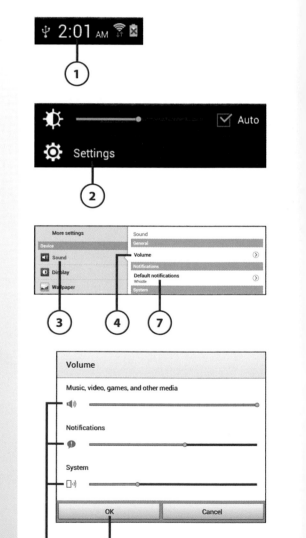

8. Set the notification ringtone from the menu. This ringtone plays whenever you receive a notification. If you don't want a ringtone, scroll to the top of the list and tap Silent.

9. Tap OK.

10. Tap Touch Sounds to play a sound when you make a screen selection.

11. Tap Screen Lock Sound to play sounds when you lock and unlock the screen.

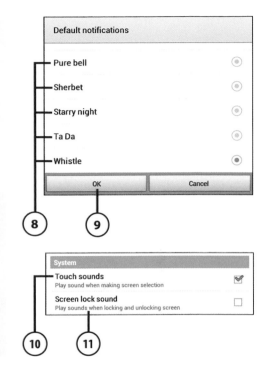

Changing Keyboard and Voice Settings

The Galaxy Tab 2 7" comes with two keyboards activated by default: the Samsung keyboard and the Swype keyboard. The Galaxy Tab 2 10" gives you more input options: the Android keyboard, the Samsung keyboard, and the TalkBack keyboard, which enables you to use your voice to manipulate the Galaxy Tab 2.

The examples in this book use keyboard settings for the Samsung keyboard, which is the default keyboard the Galaxy Tab 2 uses when you type text, as well as built-in keyboard settings that apply to all keyboards.

1. Tap the clock in the Notification bar.

2. Tap Settings.

3. Scroll down the Settings list and then tap Language and Input.

4. Because the default is the Samsung keyboard, tap the settings icon to the right of Samsung Keyboard.

5. Tap Input Language if you want to change the default keyboard input language.

6. Slide the Predictive Text slider to off (the slider turns from a green bar with an I to a gray bar with a O) if you don't want the Galaxy Tab 2 to guess what you're typing and provide you with suggestions for words so you don't have to keep typing all the time. This is similar to the auto-complete feature in word processors.

7. Tap Continuous Input to enter text by sliding the finger across the keyboard to type words. After you release your finger the word that the Galaxy Tab 2 thinks you're trying to type appears on the screen.

8. Tap Voice Input to use voice input instead of the keyboard.

9. Tap Auto Capitalization to turn off auto-capitalization for words. By default, the Galaxy Tab 2 auto-capitalizes the first word in a sentence. If the Galaxy Tab 2 recognizes a punctuation mark and a space, the next letter is capitalized automatically unless you tap the Shift key to turn it off.

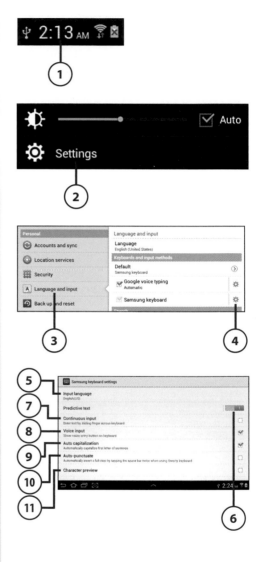

(There are exceptions to this rule, such as when you type in the To box when you compose a new email message.) You can turn the feature back on by tapping Auto Capitalization.

10. Tap Auto-Punctuate to automatically insert a full stop after a word by double-tapping the space bar.

11. Tap Character Preview to display the character you're typing on the keyboard in a box above the key for about a second after you tap the key.

12. Tap Key-Tap Sound to have the Galaxy Tab 2 make a sound each time you press a key.

13. Tap Tutorial to get a quick and easy tutorial about how to use the keyboard.

14. If you change your mind after you make settings and decide you want the default settings instead, tap Reset Settings.

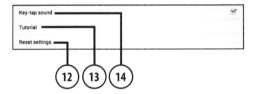

Modifying More Settings

There are too many settings in Android to cover in this book, but here are some of the more important settings that you should know about.

1. Tap the clock in the Notification bar.

2. Tap Settings.

3. Tap Display.

4. Set the brightness level by tapping Brightness and then move the slider in the Brightness window to change the brightness level. When you finish changing the brightness level, tap OK.

5. Tap Screen Timeout.

6. Select the period of inactivity after which the screen times out and goes dark. The default is one minute. If you don't want to change the time interval, tap Cancel.

Powering Up Your Screen

After the screen goes dark, you can easily start it again by tapping the screen or pressing the Power button. If your Galaxy Tab 2 is password-protected (or PIN or pattern-protected), you must type your password (or PIN or pattern) to start using the Galaxy Tab 2 again.

7. Set the font style and size by tapping Font Style and Font Size, respectively, in the Font area. When you select the font style you can choose from the built-in fonts or you can search for, purchase, and download fonts from the Google Play Store.

8. Tap Quick Launch to change the quick launch icon in the Notification bar.

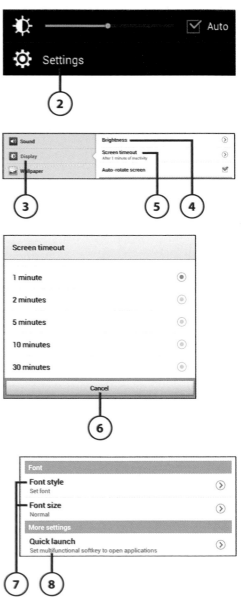

9. The default Quick Launch icon is the screen capture icon that appears to the right of the task manager icon. You can change the Quick Launch icon to launch applications, search, or the camera. If you don't want to have a Quick Launch icon, tap None. After you tap the icon in the list, the icon in the Notification bar changes (or disappears after you tap None) to reflect your choice. If you change your mind and don't want to change the icon, tap Cancel.

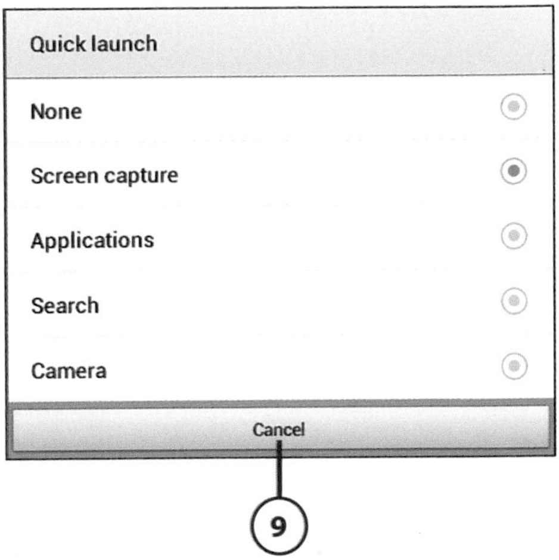

Quick launch

None

Screen capture

Applications

Search

Camera

Cancel

9

Learn how to browse
the Web and view
websites using the
built-in Internet app

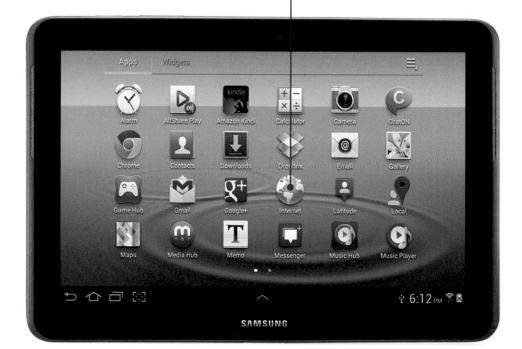

The Galaxy Tab 2 is a great tool for viewing web pages, whether you're at home or you're on the go. No matter which Galaxy Tab 2 model you use, the screen is much larger than a mobile phone so you can see more on the Galaxy Tab 2's screen. Because you can touch the screen, you can interact with web content in ways that a computer typically cannot. This chapter covers the following:

→ Browsing to a URL

→ Searching the Web

→ Viewing web pages

→ Bookmarking websites

→ Returning to previously visited websites

→ Deleting bookmarks

→ Filling in web forms

→ Copying text and images from web pages

Browsing the Web

Browsing to a URL

It's likely that you already know how to browse to different web pages in your favorite web browser on your computer. The built-in Internet app in Android works much the same as the browser on your computer, but there are some differences.

1. Tap the Applications icon.

2. Tap Internet.

3. Tap the Address field at the top of the screen. The keyboard opens at the bottom of the screen so you can type a Uniform Resource Locator (URL), which can be a website name or a specific page in a website. You can also select from one of the search sites in the list that appears below the Address field.

4. Start typing a URL, such as samsung.com or play.google.com.

5. Tap Go on the keyboard when you finish typing.

Smarter Searching

As you type, terms that match the letter(s) you've added appear in the list below the Address field. As you type more letters, Android updates the list to give you what it thinks is a more accurate list of possible terms you're looking for. You can stop typing at any time and scroll down the list to view the terms and then tap the term to open the web page. For example, as you type the first five letters of "android" (without the quotes), you see that you get terms for android and a number of other results.

Tips for Typing a URL

The Internet app doesn't require you to type the "http://" or the "www." at the beginning of the URL. For example, if you type samsung.com or www.samsung.com, you still go to the Samsung home page. However, there might be some instances when you need to type in "http://" or even "https://" (for a secure web page) at the beginning of the URL. If you do, the Internet app lets you know so you can type in the "http://" or "https://" in the Address field.

Search results when you start typing the word "android" in the Address field

Searching the Web

The Internet app makes it easy for you to search the Web, so you don't need to know every URL of every web page out there (which is good considering there are literally billions of web pages). As you type, the Internet app suggests search terms you've used in the past as well as search terms that you might be looking for.

1. Tap the Applications icon.

2. Tap Internet.

3. Tap the Address field at the top of the screen. The keyboard opens at the bottom of the screen so you can type the URL. Start typing your search term. As you type, a list appears underneath the address bar with suggestions. You can stop typing at any time and scroll down the list to find your search term; tap the search term to select it and start the search.

4. If you haven't found what you're looking for, tap Go to open the Google search page.

5. The results display in a Google search results page. Tap any link to go to a page; you can also tap one of the links at the bottom of the screen to view more results.

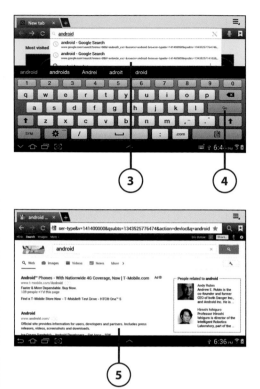

TIPS FOR SEARCHING THE WEB

>>>Go Further

You can search deeper within Google itself. For example, if you put a + in front of a search term, you're telling Google that you require the word in the search results. If you put quotes around a search term ("term"), you're telling Google that you want to search for results that contain that term. Scroll to the bottom of the search page and then tap Search Help to get more information about how you can get the most from your Google searches.

— A list of search tips from Google

If you look at the top of Google's search results page, you see links so you can search for more than text terms, including Images and Videos. If you click the More link, a pop-up list displays so you can search a variety of other areas within Google.

A list of more areas in which to search within Google

Viewing Web Pages

After you open a website, you can control what you view on the web page in several ways. These techniques let you access the entire web page and navigate between web pages in the Internet app.

1. Navigate to a web page using one of the two methods described in the previous tasks in this chapter.

2. As you view a page, you can drag up and down the page with your finger. You can also flick with your finger to scroll quickly. After you flick, the screen scrolls, decelerates, and then comes to a stop.

3. You can zoom in by double-tapping an area on the screen. Zoom out by double-tapping again.

4. While you're zoomed in, you can touch and drag left and right to view different parts of the web page.

5. Move to another web page from a link in the current web page by tapping a link. Links are usually an underlined or colored piece of text, but they can also be pictures or images that look like buttons.

Hunting for Links

Unfortunately, it isn't always easy to figure out which parts of a web page are links and which ones aren't. Back in the early days of the Web, all links were blue and underlined. As web page elements have become more enhanced over time, it's now more common to find links in any color and any text style. What's more, graphics that are links aren't underlined, either.

On a computer's web browser it's easy to find out which element is a link when you move the mouse pointer over the link because the pointer changes shape. In Android, there is no cursor, so you can't find out if a web page element is a link unless you tap it and see what happens.

Bookmarking Websites

As you browse websites, you might want to save some of the websites in a list of your favorites so you can go back to them later. In browser parlance, this saving process is called bookmarking.

1. Navigate to any page in the Internet app.

2. Tap the Add Bookmark button at the top of the page.

3. In the Bookmarks list, tap the Add Bookmark button.

4. Edit the title of the bookmark. The official title of the web page is filled in for you, but you can change the name by tapping the Name field and using the keyboard.

5. Select the folder you want to place the bookmark into by tapping Bookmarks.

6. Select the folder into which you want to place the bookmark. The default is the Bookmarks folder, but you can also select another folder or save the bookmark to the Home screen.

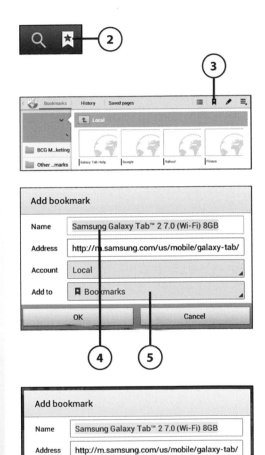

7. Tap OK.

8. The new bookmark appears in the list.

Should I Edit a Bookmark Title?

Because the titles of web pages are usually long and descriptive, it's a good idea to shorten the title to something you can recognize easily in your bookmarks list. Every bookmark also includes a thumbnail picture of what the web page looks like so you can identify the bookmark more easily. If you would rather view your bookmarks by title, press Settings and then tap List View in the menu.

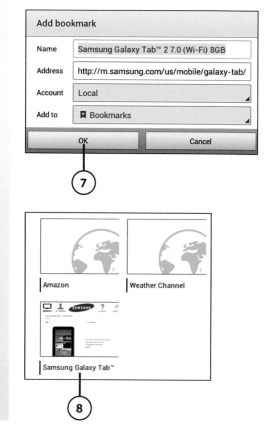

Returning to Previously Visited Pages

It's easy to return to the last page you visited in the Internet app—just press the Back button. As you keep pressing the Back button, you keep going back to pages you visited. In the History page, the Internet app also keeps a list of all web pages you've visited during your browsing session.

Browsing Forward

Like any web browser, you can browse more recent pages you've viewed in your current browsing session by tapping the Forward button, which is the right-arrow button immediately to the right of the Back button.

1. Visit several web pages in the Internet app if you haven't done so already.

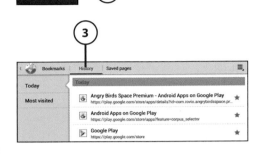

2. Tap Bookmarks.

3. Tap the History tab. The list of web pages you visited for the current date appears under the Today heading.

4. You can view web pages you visited on an earlier date by tapping the date range (such as Last 7 Days), and the list of web pages you visited displays underneath the date heading. You can also view the web pages you've visited most often by tapping Most Visited; the list displays on the right side of the screen.

Tips for Using History

If you want to hide the history for a specific day so you can see history for another day, tap the header for the specific day. For example, if you want to hide all the web pages for today, click the Today header above the first web page in the Today list. The Today header is still visible, but you won't see the web pages. You can view the web pages again by tapping the Today header.

You can also clear the entire history database by pressing Settings and then tapping the Clear History button.

Deleting Bookmarks

If you find there are websites that you don't visit anymore or that go to obsolete or missing web pages, you need to cull your bookmark list. You can delete a bookmark from the Bookmarks list or from the History list.

Delete from the Bookmarks List

The first method uses the Bookmarks list to delete a bookmark.

1. Tap the Bookmarks button at the top of the Internet screen. The thumbnail list of bookmarks appears.

2. Tap and hold your finger on the bookmark you want to delete until the pop-up menu window appears.

3. Scroll down ssthe menu until you see Delete Bookmark and then tap it.

4. A dialog box asks if you want to delete the bookmsark. Tap OK to delete the bookmark instantly.

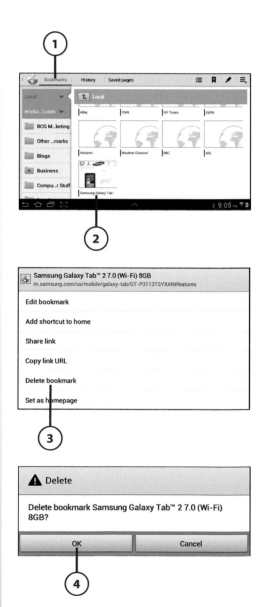

Delete from the History List

The second method uses the History list to delete a bookmark.

1. Tap the Bookmarks button at the top of the Internet screen. The thumbnail list of bookmarks appears.

2. Tap the History tab. This brings up a list of web pages you've viewed recently.

3. Tap a yellow star to the right of a website that you've viewed recently. The yellow star indicates that the site is bookmarked. After you tap the star, the Internet app immediately deletes the bookmark.

History	Saved pages	≡,

Today

Angry Birds Space Premium - Android Apps on Google Play
https://play.google.com/store/apps/details?id=com.rovio.angrybirdsspace.pr... ★

Sync Your Bookmarks

You can sync the bookmarks in your favorite web browser on your desktop or laptop computer with the Internet app so you have maximum control over your bookmarks. You can learn more about syncing your Galaxy Tab 2 in Chapter 3, "Setting Up the Galaxy Tab 2."

Filling in Web Forms

On many web pages you are asked to fill in forms, such as for signing up for a company's email newsletter or to get more information about a product. Filling out web forms on your Galaxy Tab 2 is similar to filling out forms on a computer's web browser, but there are differences.

1. Navigate to a page that you know contains a form. (The sample page is at http://code.google.com/p/android/issues/entry?template=Feature%20request.)

2. Tap in a text box.

3. The keyboard appears at the bottom of the screen. Use the keyboard to type text into the box.

4. Tap the Go button when you finish typing.

5. Select an item in a pull-down menu by tapping the field.

6. Tap an item in the menu to select it. If the menu list is long, touch and drag up and down to view more selections.

7. The selected item appears in the field.

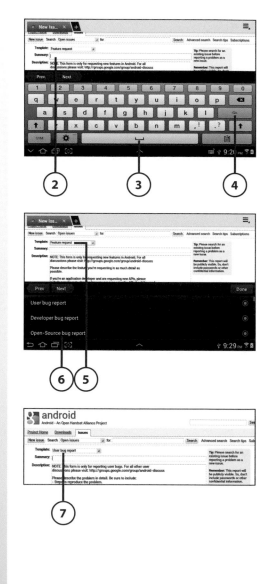

Special Menus

Some websites use special menus that are built from scratch. In these cases, the menu looks exactly like the one you get when you view the web page on a computer. If the web page is well constructed, it should work fine on the Galaxy Tab 2. However, it might be a little more difficult to make a selection.

Copying Text and Images from Web Pages

The Internet app treats web pages like other documents. That is, you can copy text and images from a web page you view in a browser to another app.

Copying a Block of Text

You can select text from web pages to copy and paste into other documents such as email messages or your own text documents.

1. Navigate to a web page in the Internet app if you haven't done so already.

2. Hold down your finger on the first word in the block of text and then release your finger. The first word is highlighted in blue with "handles" at the beginning and end of the word.

3. Hold down your finger on the bottom handle (the one on the right side of the word) and drag over the text you want to copy. When finished, release your finger. The selected text is highlighted in blue.

4. In the menu bar at the top of the screen, tap Copy.

5. Android informs you that the text has been copied to the clipboard. You can now go to another application, such as Email (or an email form on another web page), and paste the text into a text area.

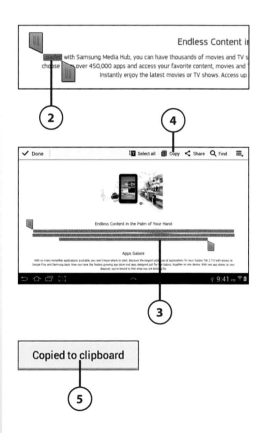

Copying an Image

In addition to being able to copy and paste text from the Internet app, you can also copy images from a web page and save them to an email message or a photo collection.

1. Go to a web page that includes an image on the page.

2. Tap and hold your finger on that image for a couple of seconds and then release your finger.

3. A pop-up menu for the image appears. Tap Save Image. This saves your image to the Photos app so you can view and use it in any app where you select images from your photo albums.

4. The downloaded file appears as an icon in the Notification bar.

5. Tap the clock in the Notification bar.

6. Scroll down the notification area and then tap the image filename to open the file in the Gallery app.

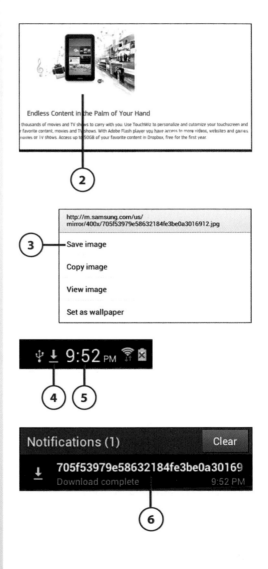

Endless Content in the Palm of Your Hand

thousands of movies and TV shows to carry with you. Use TouchWiz to personalize and customize your touchscreen and r favorite content, movies and TV shows. With Adobe Flash player you have access to more videos, websites and games. movies or TV shows. Access up to 50GB of your favorite content in Dropbox, free for the first year.

2

http://m.samsung.com/us/
mirror/400x/705f53979e58632184fe3be0a3016912.jpg

3 — Save image

Copy image

View image

Set as wallpaper

⚡ ↓ 9:52 PM 📶 ✕

4 **5**

Notifications (1)   Clear

↓ 705f53979e58632184fe3be0a30169
   Download complete   9:52 PM

6

7. In the Gallery app screen, tap the Menu icon.

8. Tap See All. You can share your image through a Bluetooth device or in an instant message. You learn more about Bluetooth in Chapter 13, "Adding New Hardware," and more about instant messaging in Chapter 6, "Sending Email and Instant Messages."

Send and receive
email from your ISP
or an email service

Send and receive
instant messages

Your Galaxy Tab 2 makes it easy for you to read and respond to email messages when you're on the go. Before you start, though, you need to configure your email account(s) and then figure out how to use the built-in Email app. Email isn't the only way to communicate. The Galaxy Tab 2 also contains a built-in Messaging app so you can configure your instant message settings to communicate using standard text message (SMS) and multimedia message (MMS) services. This chapter covers the following topics:

→ Configuring and reading email
→ Composing a new message
→ Deleting and moving messages
→ Searching through email
→ Configuring email settings
→ Sending and receiving instant messages

Sending Email and Instant Messages

Configuring Email

Following is a complete checklist of the information you need to set up your Galaxy Tab 2 to use a traditional email account. If you have an email service such as Exchange, Google Gmail, or Yahoo! you won't need all this. However, if you don't configure the email settings, you can't use webmail services in other apps (like Gmail) to do things such as email web page links or photos, so you need some of the following information no matter what:

- Email address
- Account type (POP or IMAP)
- Incoming mail server address
- Incoming mail user ID
- Incoming mail password
- Outgoing mail server address
- Outgoing mail user ID
- Outgoing mail password

>>>Go Further

DO I USE POP OR IMAP?

If you're not sure whether to use POP or IMAP as your account type, keep the following in mind:

Post Office Protocol, or POP, retrieves and removes email from a server. Therefore, the server acts as a temporary holding place for email. If you receive email using both your Galaxy Tab 2 and your computer, it's more difficult to share your email messages using POP. You need to either set up your email to go to one device and some to another device, or you need to set up one device so it doesn't remove email from the server so another device can retrieve the email as well.

Internet Message Access Protocol, or IMAP, makes the server the place where all messages are stored. Your Galaxy Tab 2 and computer display all email messages on the server. This is the better situation if you have multiple devices retrieving email from the same account.

1. On the Home screen, swipe your finger from left to right to view more app icons.

2. Tap the Email icon.

3. In the Set Up Email screen, type the email address in the highlighted Email Address field. When you start typing, the keyboard appears at the bottom of the screen.

4. Tap Next in the keyboard.

5. Tap the password for your email account in the Password field. As you type in the password characters, they become dots so the password is hidden right away.

6. Tap Next.

7. Tap the button that corresponds to the account type you have.

8. Type the incoming server settings into the appropriate fields.

9. Tap Next.

10. After the Galaxy Tab 2 checks your incoming server settings, type the outgoing server settings into the appropriate fields.

11. Tap Next.

12. In the Account Options screen, the default is for the Galaxy Tab 2 to notify you when email arrives. Automatically download files attached to email messages by tapping the check box.

13. Change the checking frequency by tapping the Email Check Frequency field. The default frequency is to check your inbox every 15 minutes. You can have the Tab check for new email as often as every 5 minutes. If that's too often, you can have the Tab check every 10 minutes, 15 minutes, 30 minutes, every hour, every 4 hours, or once per day. You can turn off email checking by tapping Never.

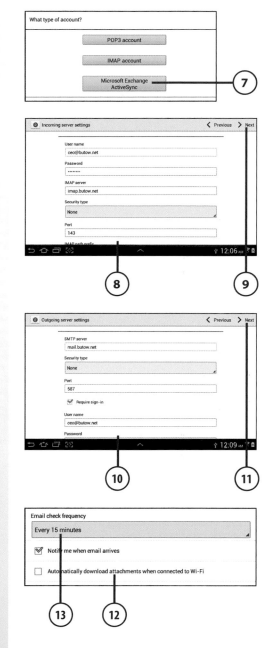

14. Tap the checking frequency in the list.

15. Tap Next.

16. In the Set Up Email page, type an optional name into the Give This Account a Name field.

17. Type your name as you want it to be displayed in outgoing messages.

18. Tap Done. A list of your email messages appears in your Inbox screen.

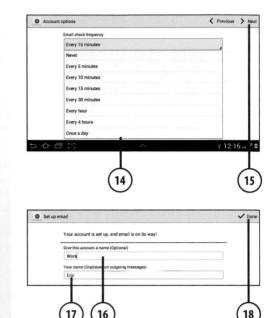

What Happens if the Settings Won't Verify?

If your settings don't verify, a dialog box displays, asking you to tap the Edit Details button to return to the previous screen and double-check all the information you entered. When something is wrong, it often comes down to misspelled information, such as a misspelled word or a letter that needs to be capitalized, or other incorrect information, such as a different outgoing server port number.

The Refresh icon

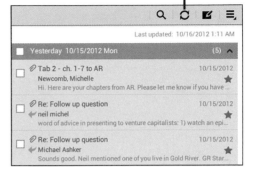

Can I Still Check My Mail Even if the App Never Checks Mail Automatically?

You can still check your mail list by tapping the Refresh icon in the Inbox screen as shown in the figure. After you tap the Refresh icon, the app checks for new messages. Any new messages appear at the top of the Inbox.

Reading Email

You use the Email app to navigate, read, and type your email messages. Let's begin by reading some email messages.

1. Tap the Apps icon on the Home screen and then tap Email.

2. Your list of Inbox folder messages appears with a list of folders to the left of the message. Tap a message in the list to view it. New messages appear with the subject line in bold type. A folder you're currently in is highlighted in blue in the folder list.

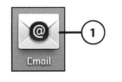

3. Tap the envelope icon at the top-left corner of the screen to return to your list of messages and folders.

4. Tap the sender's name at the top of the page.

5. Tap Create Contact to add the sender to your list of contacts.

6. Tap the account you want to add the contact to. The Create Contact window opens.

7. Type information into the Create Contact screen fields if you want. (You learn more about adding a contact in Chapter 7, "Using the Calendar and Contacts to Simplify Your Life.") Tap Save to save the new contact and return to the message list.

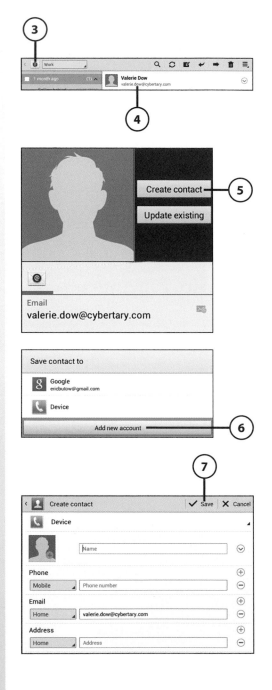

8. Tap the email account name in the upper-left corner of the screen and then tap the account name in the list.

9. Scroll down the folder list to view folders within the Inbox and tap a folder to view messages within that folder.

10. The list of messages within that folder appears to the right of the folder list.

11. Scroll up the folder list until you see the Inbox folder. Tap it.

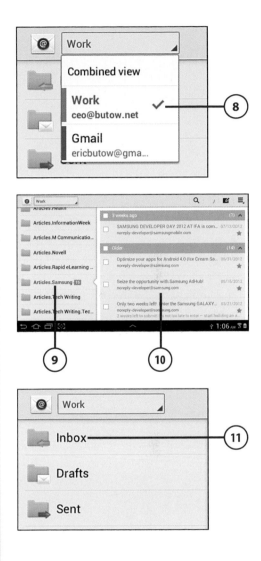

12. Tap a message in the list.

13. Tap the Refresh icon to refresh the message list on the left side of the screen. Any new messages that have come in appear at the top of the list.

How Do You Create Folders?

You can't create folders inside your mailbox in the Email app. If you use an IMAP mail server, you can go to the web interface for that server and create a new folder there so it appears in the Email app. Unfortunately, if you use a POP email server, you cannot add folders to the server—all you have is Inbox, Sent, and Trash.

How Do I Combat Spam?

The Galaxy Tab has no spam filter built in. However, most email servers filter spam at the server level. If you use a basic POP or IMAP account from an ISP, unfortunately you might not have any server-side spam filtering. If you use an account at a service such as Gmail, you get spam filtering on the server, and spam mail goes to the Junk folder, not your Inbox.

Composing a New Message

The process for composing a new message and composing a reply to a message is similar. This section covers composing a message from scratch.

1. In the Email app, tap the New Mail button.

2. Enter the recipient's address in the To field.

3. Tap +Cc/Bcc to enter an address so you can copy (Cc) or blind copy (Bcc) the message.

4. Tap +Send Email to Myself if you'd like to send a copy of the message to your own email address so that you have a record of what you sent.

5. Tap in the Subject field and then type a subject for the email.

6. Tap below the Subject field in the body of the email and then type your message.

7. Tap Send.

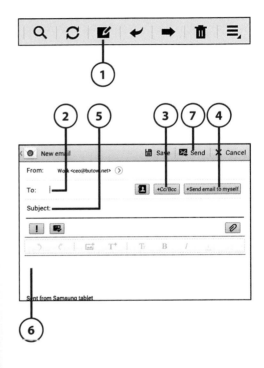

Add Attachments

If you've copied text or images to your clipboard, you can add that text or image as an attachment, just as you can with any email program on your computer. Just tap the Attach button, which has a paper clip icon and is located underneath the subject line near the far right of the window. Then you can pick your text, image(s), contacts, or location from the Attach window.

Creating Your Own Signature

You can create a signature that automatically appears at the end of your messages. You create your signature in the Email app.

1. On the Apps screen, tap the Email icon.

2. Tap the Menu button.

3. Tap Settings.

4. Tap your account name in the list.

5. Tap Signature.

6. Type what you want the signature to say (such as your full name) in the Signature field.

7. Tap OK.

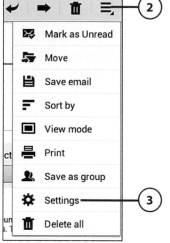

8. The signature as it will appear in your Message Composition field appears under the Signature heading.

Signature
Eric Butow

⑧

Can I Have Multiple Signatures?

You can have only one signature per email account on your Galaxy Tab 2, so technically you can't have multiple signatures. However, the signature is placed in the editable area of the Message Composition field, so you can edit it like the rest of your message and create multiple signatures that way.

Deleting Messages

When you view a message, you can tap the Delete icon and move the message to the trash.

1. In the Email app, go to any mailbox and any subfolder, such as your Inbox.

2. Tap a check box at the left side of the message entry that you want to delete.

3. Tap the Trash icon.

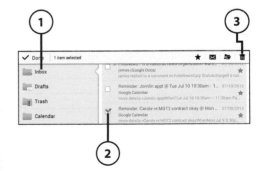

4. Tap a check box at the left side of the message entry in the list. You can select multiple check boxes if you want to delete multiple messages.

5. Tap the Trash icon to delete the selected messages.

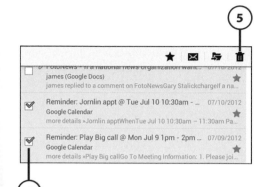

Can I Move Messages to Other Folders?

Unfortunately, you can't move messages in the Email app from one folder to another. If you use an IMAP server, you can log in to the web interface for that server and move messages around there. The next time you log in to the Email app, the app reflects the changes you made in the IMAP server. If you're using a POP server, though, the only way you can move messages is to do so in another email program like one on your desktop or laptop computer.

Searching Through Email

By default, the Galaxy Tab 2 doesn't let you search through your email messages. You can change this quickly and then search text in your email messages.

1. In the Apps screen, tap Email.

2. Tap the Search icon.

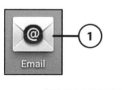

3. Tap All and then choose whether you want to search for the term in the entire message (All), just the sender name, or just the title of the message. All is the default.

4. Type the search term into the Search Email field.

5. As you type, updated results display below the field. In my example, I typed `fols` into the field and the Folsom Chamber LLL meeting subject appears in the list. Tap a message to open it.

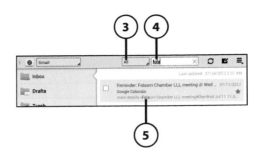

What's the Continue Searching on Server Link?

If you use an IMAP server, you can search other locations on your server (such as other email accounts) for the search term you entered by tapping the Continue Searching on Server link. After you tap this link, more results (if any) appear underneath your original search results. If you use another type of email service, such as POP, you won't see this link.

Configuring Email Settings

The Galaxy Tab enables you to update your email account settings as needed.

1. Follow the steps from earlier tasks in this chapter to open the Email app if you aren't there already. Then tap the Menu icon.

2. Tap Settings.

3. Tap your account in the Account Manager list if there is more than one. If not, your account appears on the screen automatically.

4. Change your account name by tapping Account Name.

5. Add or change your name by tapping Your Name.

6. Add or change your signature by tapping Signature as you did earlier in this chapter.

7. Tap Default Account if you don't want to send email from this account by default. Scroll down for more options.

8. If you always want to add your email address in the Cc or Bcc box, tap Always Cc/Bcc Myself and then select Cc or Bcc in the pop-up window.

9. By default, the Forward with Files check box is checked so when you forward a message that has file attachments, those attachments are also included in your forwarded message. Turn this feature off by tapping the check box. Scroll down for more options.

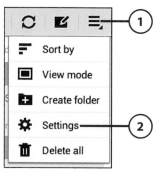

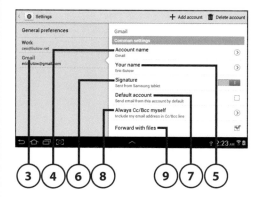

10. The Email app shows the 25 most recent messages within a folder's message list by default. You can change this by tapping Recent Messages and then selecting the number of recent messages in the pop-up window. You can choose from 25 messages up to all messages in the folder.

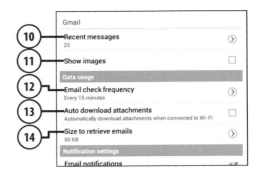

11. Tap Show Images to automatically show images in a message when you view it.

12. Change the email checking frequency by tapping Email Check Frequency as you did earlier in this chapter.

13. Tap Auto Download Attachments to download file attachments in a message to the app automatically.

14. When you receive messages, the Email app only downloads the first 50KB of data in a message by default. If the message has more than 50KB of data then at the bottom of the message the app asks if you want to download the rest of the message. Tap Size to Retrieve Emails to open the pop-up window and change the default amount of data you can receive in an email message. You can choose from 2KB to 100KB. Scroll down to view more options.

15. Tap Email Notifications to specify whether the Galaxy Tab 2 should notify you when email arrives. This feature is activated by default. Deactivate it by tapping the check box.

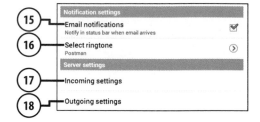

16. Select a ringtone, or no ringtone at all, by tapping Select Ringtone and then selecting the ringtone from the Select Ringtone pop-up window. The default ringtone is Postman.

17. Change your incoming settings (as you did with a new account earlier in this chapter) by tapping Incoming Settings.

18. Change your outgoing settings (as you did with a new account earlier in this chapter) by tapping Outgoing Settings.

Sending and Receiving Instant Messages

You can send and receive instant messages using one of two built-in apps: The Messenger app and the Google Talk app. If you communicate with Google Talk users then use the Google Talk app. The Messenger app connects to other Google+ users.

Messenger App

The first time you use the Messenger app, you see different screens than what you'll see after you set up the app.

First Use

1. Tap the Applications icon.

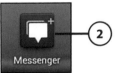

2. Tap Messenger.

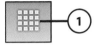

3. If you already have an existing Google account, tap the account name in the list within the Select an Account window. The Messenger app logs you in, and you might be asked to choose an account if you have more than one Google+ account assigned to your name. If you do then tap the appropriate account in the Choose Account list before tapping the Next button.

Can I Use a Different Google Account?

If you have more than one Google account, you can use that by tapping the Add Account button in the Select an account window. Then you can tap the Existing button to sign in using the Google account email address and password.

---

4. Tap the New Message icon.

5. Type your message in the Add a Comment box.

6. By default, your message is sent to everyone in your circles on Google+. Change this by tapping the Circles icon.

7. In the Share With screen, tap one or more circle names to select or deselect the circles to which you want to send your message.

8. Scroll down to tap the name of the contact or contacts to whom you want to send the message. After you tap the name, the check box to the right of the name is checked.

9. When you're done, tap OK.

10. Tap the location icon to change or hide your location.

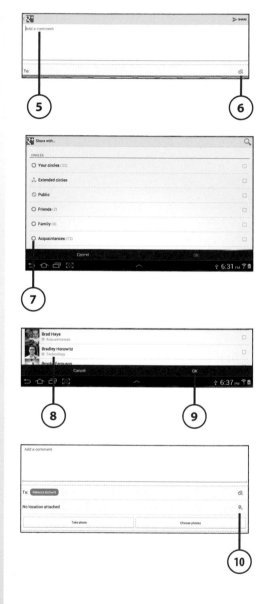

11. In the Share Your Location screen you can hide the location in your message, choose your current location (which is the default selection), change your location to your city, or select a different landmark in your city or town as your location.

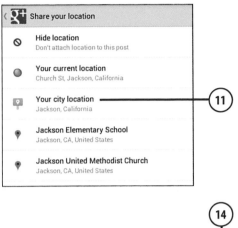

12. Tap Take Photo to open the Camera app and take a photo on the Galaxy Tab 2 to include with your message. You find out more about the Camera app in Chapter 10, "Capturing and Managing Photos."

13. Tap Choose Photos to choose a photo stored on your Galaxy Tab 2 from within the selection screen.

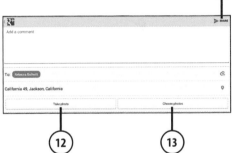

14. When you're finished creating your message, tap Share.

Using Messenger After Setup

The next time you open Messenger after you set it up, you see different screens so you can start a conversation with anyone or any of your circles.

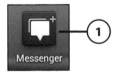

1. In the Apps screen, tap Messenger.

2. Tap the person in the list to whom you want to start a message conversation.

3. For this example, tap the New Message icon.

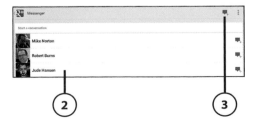

4. Type the name, email address, or circle name.

5. Tap the plus icon to select the circles or names in the Add People screen.

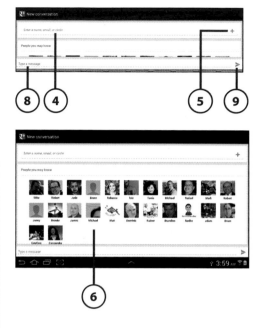

6. In the People You May Know section, type the name of the person with whom you want to chat. The person's name appears at the top of the screen.

7. Continue tapping names of people you want to include in the conversation. If you want to delete the person's name from the conversation, tap the person's name.

8. Tap type a message and type your message in the box.

9. Tap the send icon to send your message. The app replaces the People You May know section with your messages and the responses from the other person(s) in the conversation.

Google Talk App

1. In the Apps screen, swipe your finger from right to left to view the second page within the screen. Tap Talk.

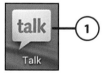

2. Tap your user ID in the screen.

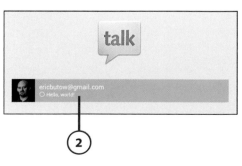

3. Tap the Status Message box.

4. Type a new status message in the Status Message box.

5. Tap Save.

6. Tap Available to change the availability status others see in Google Talk. The options are Available, Busy, and Invisible. You can also sign out of Google Talk.

7. Tap Change to a Recently-Used Status to view a history of your recent status updates. You can also clear your status history.

What if I Don't Use Either Google+ or Google Talk for Instant Messaging?

If you use a different instant messaging service then visit the Google Play Store by tapping Play Store on the Home screen. Then search for the instant messaging app you're looking for. If you use Skype, for example, there is a Skype app for Android available that you can download free of charge. You discover more about downloading apps in Chapter 12, "Enhancing Your Galaxy Tab 2 with Apps."

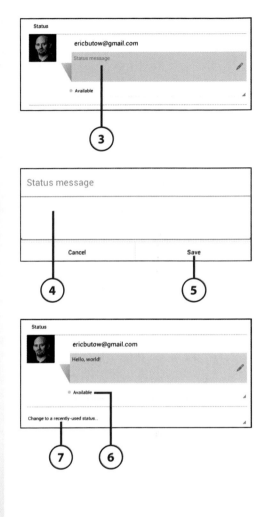

Configuring Messenger Settings

You can't change Messenger app settings after you set it up for the first time. The next time you log on, you can change your settings so you can manage your messages to your liking and determine how you want to be notified of new messages that come into your message Inbox.

1. In the Apps screen, tap Messenger.

2. Tap the Menu icon.

3. Tap Settings.

4. Tap Messenger.

5. By default, the Messenger Notifications check box is selected so notifications appear in the status bar at the top of the screen. Turn this feature off by tapping Messenger notifications.

6. Tap Ringtone to change the ringtone that sounds when you receive messages.

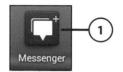

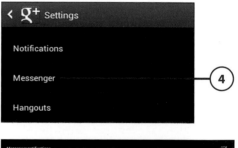

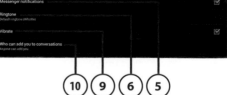

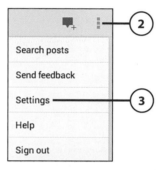

7. You can select from the default ringtone, a number of other ringtones, or silent mode.

8. After you select the ringtone, tap OK.

9. The Vibrate check box is checked by default, which means the Galaxy Tab 2 vibrates when you receive a notification. Turn the vibration off by tapping Vibrate.

10. By default, any of your contacts can add you to conversations they're having. If you want to restrict who can add you, tap Who Can Add You to Conversations.

11. Tap Your circles to give only contacts in your circles the ability to add you to conversations. If you want people in your contacts' circles to add you to conversations, tap Extended Circles.

Ringtone	
Default ringtone	◉
Silent	◉
Bubbles	◉
Charming bell	◉
Cheeper	◉
OK	Cancel

8 **7**

Who can add you to conversations	
Anyone	◉
Your circles	◉
Extended circles	◉
Cancel	

11

Configuring Google Talk Settings

You can change your instant message settings in Google Talk's settings screen so you can manage your messages to your liking, set Cell Broadcast settings, and determine how you want to be notified of new messages that come into your message Inbox.

1. Tap Talk in the Apps screen.

2. Tap the Menu icon.

3. Tap Settings.

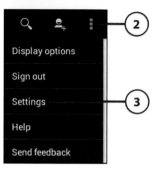

4. Tap Mobile Indicator if you want to show your Google Talk friends that you're on a mobile device when you're talking to them.

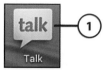

5. By default, Google Talk sets the status to Away when your screen turns off. If you want your status to remain the same regardless of your screen status, tap Away When Screen Off to clear the check box.

6. Tap Invitations Notifications to turn off the feature that notifies you when a friend invites you to chat on Google Talk.

7. Tap IM Notifications to change how you want the Galaxy Tab to notify you when you receive a new message. The default is a system bar notification, but you can also have the system open a dialog box or turn notifications off.

8. Tap Notification Ringtone to change the ringtone that sounds when you receive messages.

9. Change how you want to have the system notify you of a video chat request by tapping Video Chat Notifications. You can either have the system open a dialog box (the default) or notify you on the system bar. Scroll down to see more options.

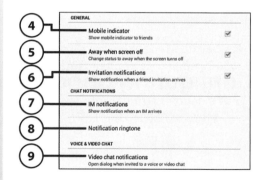

10. Tap Video Chat Ringtone to change the video chat request ringtone. Choose a ringtone from the list.

11. Tap Default Video Effect to set the video stabilization. The default is Low, but you can improve video stabilization by choosing the stabilization option in the Image Stabilization window list.

12. Tap Blocked Friends to view all friends you have.

13. Tap Clear Search History to clear all previous Google Talk chat searches in Google Talk's search box.

14. Tap Manage Account to open the Accounts and Sync page within the Settings screens so you can manage sync information with your Google services.

15. Tap Terms & Privacy to open a Browser window and view terms and privacy information for Google Talk.

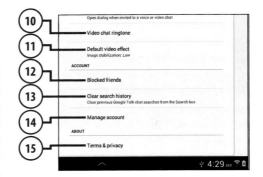

Store and search all
your contacts

Monitor the day's weather,
news, and track stocks from
one convenient location

Track your appointments
and events

In this chapter, you find out how to organize your daily schedule, news, and information. You also learn how to add and search contacts and calendar events. Topics in this chapter include:

→ Choosing a weather forecast for your briefing
→ Tracking stocks
→ Selecting your news settings
→ Checking and adding to your personal schedule
→ Setting up contacts accounts
→ Managing contacts
→ Using contacts
→ Creating calendar events
→ Using calendar views

7

Using the Calendar and Contacts to Simplify Your Life

Your Samsung Galaxy is highly capable of helping you organize your busy life. The preinstalled Contacts and Calendar widgets help you improve your daily efficiency by enabling you to manage personal contacts and schedule important appointments. You can also download free productivity apps from the Google Play Store to get the latest weather forecast, learn what's happening on the stock market, and view the latest news stories. Let's take a close look at what these productivity apps, as well as the Contacts and Calendar widgets, can do for you.

Staying Up to Date

If you want to stay up to date with news, weather, and stock information, there are several well-reviewed free apps available in the Google Play Store.

- AccuWeather, which is an app that allows you to get up to the minute weather conditions and forecasts for your area.

- The Stock Alert Tablet Edition app enables you to view all sorts of information about stocks.

- If you're looking for news, search for News360 for Tablets.

This section gives you a brief look at these three apps so you can get the information you're looking for on your Galaxy Tab 2. Start by downloading the apps. (You can find out how to download apps in Chapter 12, "Enhancing Your Galaxy Tab 2 with Apps.") You can also explore the Google Play Store to see what other apps might meet your needs.

Choosing a Weather Forecast

Follow these steps to display the forecast for a specific city in AccuWeather:

1. Tap Play Store on the Home screen.

2. Tap the Search icon.

3. Start typing AccuWeather in the Search field.

4. Tap accuweather in the search list.

5. Tap AccuWeather in the Apps page.

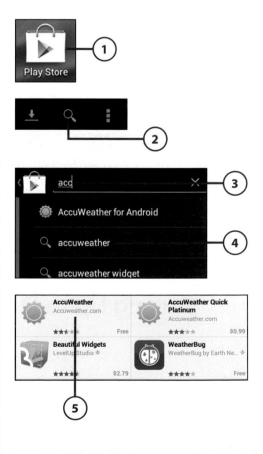

6. Tap Install.

7. Tap Accept & Download.

8. After the Galaxy Tab 2 downloads and installs the app, tap Open.

9. Tap I Agree on the Terms and Conditions screen.

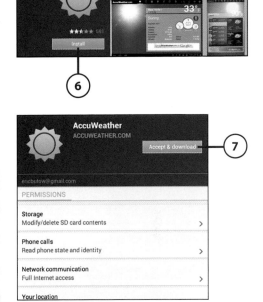

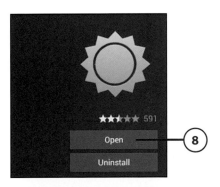

10. Type your location in the form of City, State (like Jackson CA) into the Add Location box, and then tap the Search button.

11. The current conditions appear on the screen.

12. Tap the Current icon.

13. Tap the Forecast icon to view the 15-day forecast.

14. You can scroll down the days to see the forecasted conditions for the next 15 days.

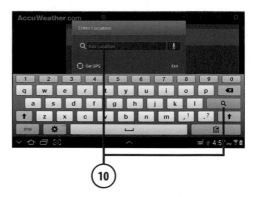

Adding Additional Forecasts

You can add additional forecasts by tapping Locations in the top-right corner of the screen; then tap Add Location and type in a new city. You can navigate among the multiple forecasts by tapping Locations and then selecting the location from the Locations list.

Updating Forecasts and Other Settings

By default, you must manually refresh the weather forecast by tapping the Refresh icon at the upper-right area of the screen. You can further customize your forecasts by tapping Settings at the far upper-right corner of the screen, such as changing the units and time format.

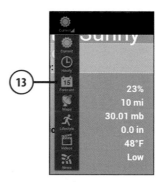

Tracking Stocks

You can configure the Stock Alert Tablet app so that you can monitor a desired stock for a company.

1. Tap Play Store on the Home screen.

2. Tap the Search icon.

3. Type stock alert in the Search field.

4. Tap stock alert in the list.

5. Tap Stock Alert Tablet Edition on the Apps screen.

6. Tap Install.

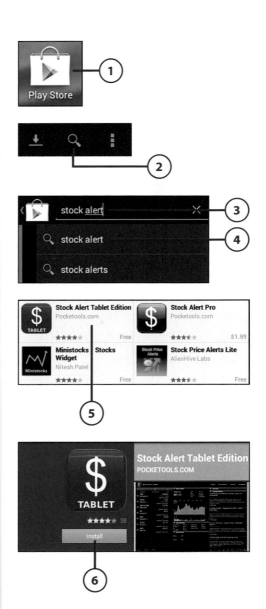

7. Tap Accept & Download. The Galaxy Tab 2 downloads and installs the Stock Alert Tablet Edition app automatically.

8. After the Galaxy Tab 2 downloads and installs the app, tap Open.

Launching Stock Alert Tablet Edition from the Home Screen

After you install the Stock Alert Tablet Edition app, the system installs a link icon on the Home screen. On the Home screen, you need to swipe twice from left to right to open the Home screen page that contains the app icon. Tap this icon to launch the app from the Home screen the next time you want to run it.

9. If this is your first time starting Stock Alert Tablet, tap Accept to accept the End User agreement.

10. Tap the Add Stock icon to add a stock.

11. Type the name of the company with the stock that you want to track. You can also type the stock ticker name.

12. Tap Search to view a list of results for the stock.

13. Scroll down the stock list in the window if necessary. Tap the name of the stock that you just added to view the stock summary.

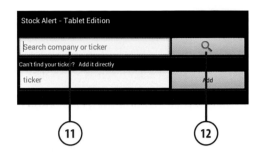

Adding Additional Stocks

You can add an additional stock by tapping the Add Stock icon, typing in a new stock ticker in the ticker box directly underneath the Search box, and then tapping Add. You can navigate between multiple stocks by scrolling up and down your list of stocks in the left column and then tapping the stock you want to view.

Refreshing Stocks

By default, your stock information must be manually refreshed by tapping the Refresh Rates icon above the list of stocks in the left column on the screen.

Selecting Your News Settings

You can browse the latest world, national, and local news stories by customizing your news settings in News360. However, before you can do so you need to create a News360 account.

1. Tap Play Store on the Home screen.

2. Tap the Search icon.

3. Type News360 in the Search field.

4. Tap news360 in the list.

5. Tap News360 for Tablets on the Apps screen.

6. Tap Install.

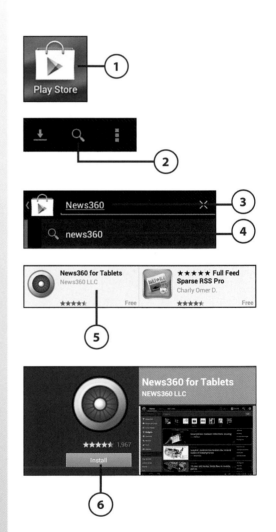

7. Tap Accept & Download. The Galaxy Tab 2 downloads and installs the News360 for Tablets app automatically.

8. After the Galaxy Tab 2 downloads and installs the app, tap Open.

9. Tap Sign In to sign in with an existing social networking account.

10. Choose how you want to authenticate with News360 by tapping the appropriate social networking website icon. You can use your Facebook, Twitter, Google+, or email account information. This example uses a connection through a Facebook account.

11. In the Facebook screen, type your email account and password, and then tap Log In.

12. Tap category names that you want to add to News360. Swipe to the left to view more categories, and as you tap each category name the selected categories appear at the top of the screen.

13. When you finish adding categories, tap Build News360.

14. The opening screen shows you some important features of the News360 screen and how to use the app. Tap Got It, Continue.

15. You can learn how to save stories to the Galaxy Tab 2, mark stories as interesting, and sync news stories on other devices and the Web. After you review the information on the screen, tap Start using News360.

16. Above the default list of stories on the home page, the list of your interest categories appears in the category bar. Swipe left and right within the bar to view all categories in the list. Tap one of the categories to view stories within that category under the category bar. If there are no stories in the category, News360 invites you to return later.

17. Tap Top Stories.

18. The list of top stories appears. You can scroll up and down the list and tap a story title to read it.

Viewing Subcategories

If a category has subcategories underneath it, then those subcategories will appear in the category bar. The category appears at the left side of the bar (to the right of the Back icon) and you'll see subcategories to the right of that category. For example, in the Science category there are subcategories that include Space, Biology, and Math. Tap the Back icon to view the main categories again.

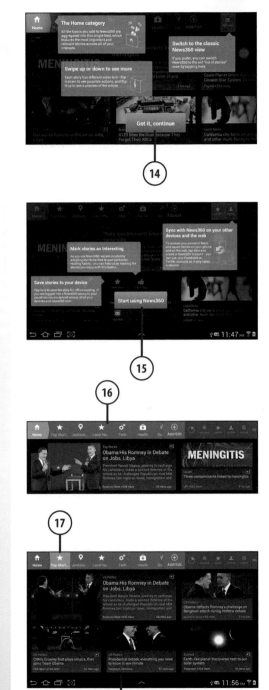

19. Options for filtering and customizing your news are located at the upper-right corner of the screen. Tap the Search icon to search for articles or topics.

20. Tap the Add/Edit icon to open the settings page.

21. Remove one of your existing categories by tapping the X button to the upper right of the category icon or by tapping a gray topic tile that has a green checkmark in the upper-right corner of the tile.

22. Add new categories by tapping a black tile. After you tap it, the tile changes color to gray and a green checkmark appears in the upper-right corner of the tile.

23. Scroll to the left and right to view more category tile screens and select new tiles.

24. Search for category topics by tapping in the Search box and then typing the search term in the box. Category tiles that most closely match your search term appear on the screen.

25. Tap a social networking website so you can connect News360 to that website and have News360 search for topics from your social networking website accounts. Websites you can select include Twitter and Google+, and you can also connect to the EverNote notetaking app and RSS feed accounts. Currently connected accounts are in full color and those that are not are grayed out.

26. Apply the changes and close the page by tapping Done. Your new category (or categories) appears in the category bar though you may need to swipe to the left within the bar to see it.

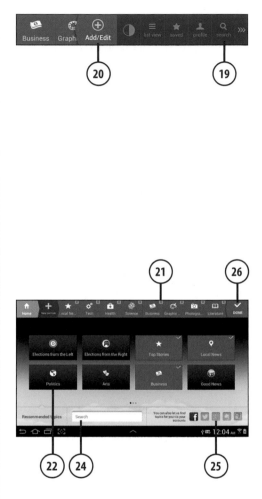

How Do I Rearrange My Categories in the Category Bar?

If you want to rearrange categories in the category bar, tap the Add/Edit icon in the bar. In the Add/Edit page, tap the category name at the top of the list, such as My Interests. Next tap and hold your finger on the category name you want to move. Drag the category name to the left or right and then release your finger when the category is in your desired location in the menu.

As you move the icon, you'll see where your icon will appear and other icons will move aside to make room for your icon. Release your finger to place the icon in that location. If you want to move your selected icon to a location in the bar that's currently not visible, move the icon to the right side of the bar. Next, swipe to the left within the bar to view the remaining icons in the bar, and then move your selected icon to the right until the icon is where you want it.

27. Tap the Profile icon.

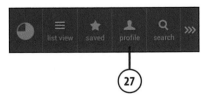

28. In the left side of the screen, swipe up and down to view your account information and sign out of News360, view social networking and app accounts to which you're connected, and to change application settings. These settings include showing or hiding high-quality images when you're connected to the Internet using a 3G connection and to show or hide pop-up messages when you earn stars. You learn more about stars starting in Step 31.

29. On the right side of the screen, swipe up and down to get more information about News360, send feedback about the app, tell friends about the app, and rate the app in the Google Play Store.

30. Return to the News360 home page by tapping Home.

31. Tap the Reading Stats icon.

32. The Your Reading Stats page shows you how many stars you've collected as you've been reading stories. Every time you read a story you receive a star. When you receive 20 stars, News360 begins to personalize the stories you see on the home page so they're in the categories you prefer.

33. Return to the home page by clicking Home.

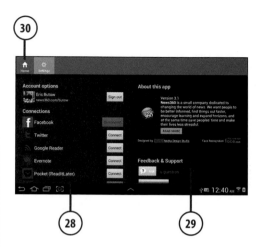

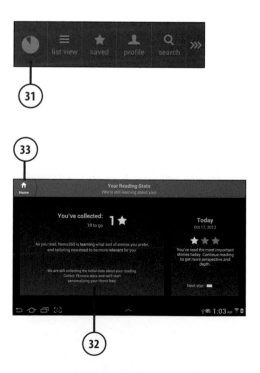

It's Not All Good

REFRESHING NEWS STORIES

By default, News360 refreshes news stories when the app finds new stories to post in your headlines list. If you want to refresh your headlines list manually, tap the category name in the category bar. After a second or two, updated stories appear in tiles on the screen.

Managing Contacts

The Contacts widget enables you to manage all the important information you receive from colleagues, friends, and prospective business associates. Think of your Galaxy Tab 2 as a virtual filing cabinet or Rolodex where you can store contact information such as names, addresses, emails, and notes. If you collect contacts with other social networking services, you can also configure Contacts to sync information between accounts.

Setting Up Contacts Accounts

The Galaxy Tab 2 can synchronize its contacts information with multiple accounts, such as Google, Corporate Exchange, other email providers, and sites such as Facebook and Google+. Information on your Galaxy Tab 2 is updated when you make changes to information in your accounts. Setting up a contacts account is quite easy.

1. Tap the clock on the Notification bar.

2. Tap Settings.

3. Tap Accounts and Sync.

4. Tap Add Account.

5. Tap an account that you would like to set up.

6. Follow the prompts to set up each account that you would like to add. The accounts you add appear in the Manage Accounts area of the Accounts and Sync Screen.

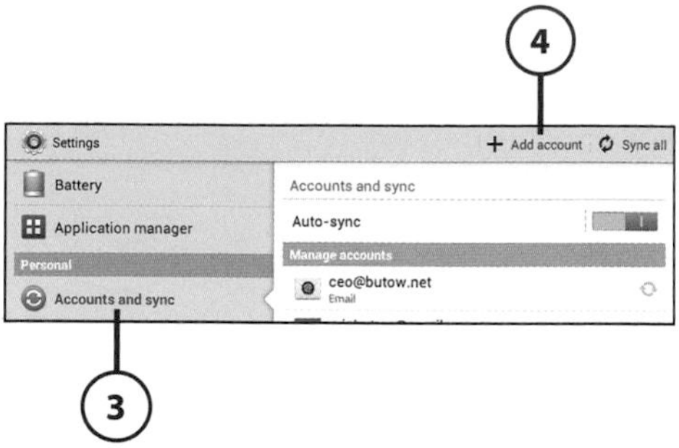

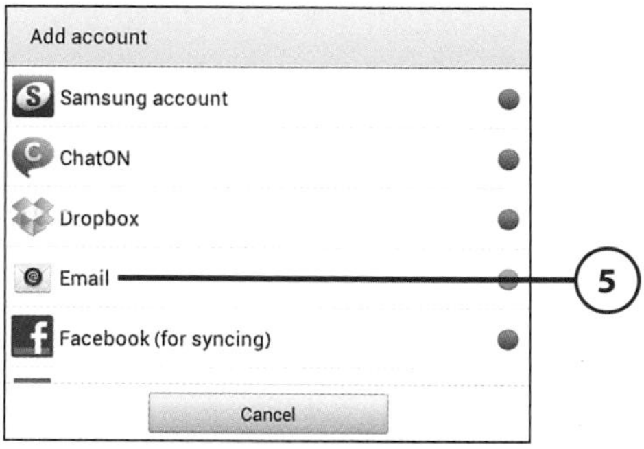

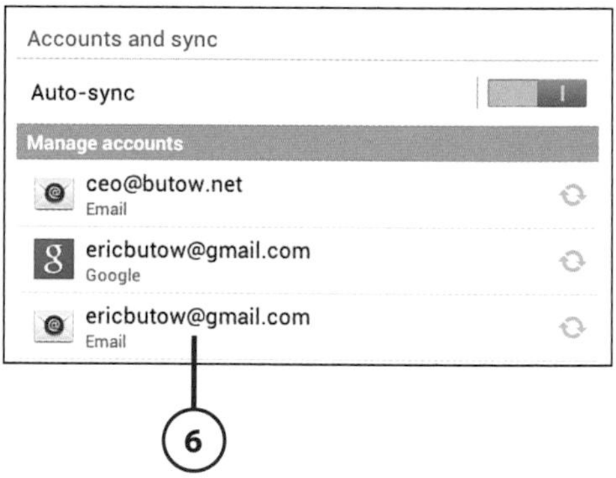

Adding Contacts

You can store contact information for family, friends, and colleagues for quick access and to send messages. Let's take a look at the Contacts widget.

1. Tap Apps on the Home screen.

2. Tap Contacts.

3. A list of all contacts appears. Your own contact information appears listed by default.

4. Tap the New button at the upper-right corner of the screen to open the Create Contact form window.

5. Tap Device to change the account for which you want to add a contact. For example, you can add a contact in your Google account.

6. Type the first and last name in the Name field.

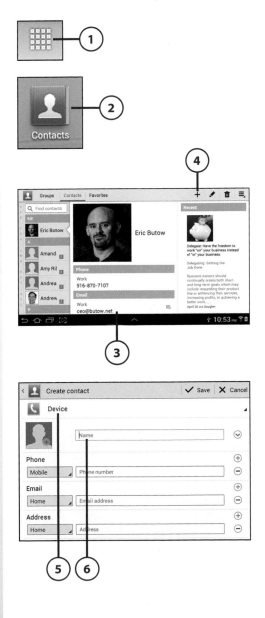

7. If you want to add the first and last name in different fields, tap the arrow icon located at the end of the Name field to add a Name Prefix, First Name, Middle Name, Last Name, and Name Suffix to the contact. There is no need to use the Shift key on the keyboard to capitalize the name because the Galaxy Tab 2 does this automatically.

8. Scroll down the window to change more fields.

Don't Worry About Formatting

You don't need to type parentheses or dashes for the phone numbers you enter. The Galaxy Tab 2 formats the number for you.

9. Tap the labels within fields to reveal a pop-up menu with other labels to choose from. Tap the label again to dismiss the pop-up list.

10. Tap the plus icon in the Phone field to add an additional field, or tap the minus icon to remove a field.

11. Add information in the Email and Address sections as you did in the Phone section.

12. Add events for the contact, such as the person's birthday, by tapping the plus icon to the right of the Events section title.

13. Tap the Birthday label to choose the type of event you want to add.

Assigning Contacts to Groups

You can assign a contact to one of three groups (Family, Friends, or Work) by tapping the Groups field located toward the bottom of the New Contact sheet and then tapping a group.

14. Add another field to the form by tapping Add Another Field. You can add the user's phonetic name, organization, instant messaging address, any notes about the user, the user's nickname, website, Internet phone number, and relationship to you.

15. Tap Save to complete the new contact.

Updating a Contact

You can update a contact by first tapping an existing contact in the Contacts list and then tapping the Edit icon located at the upper right of the screen next to the New icon. The contact sheet opens so that you can edit or add information.

Displaying Contacts

You can control how your contacts are listed by setting sorting and display preferences. After you launch the Contacts widget, you can tap the Settings icon located at the upper-right corner of the screen, tapping Settings, and then tapping Display contacts by. The Display Options menu enables you to list by First Name (which is the default setting) or by Last Name First.

Searching for Contacts

Your list of contacts is sure to grow the longer you have your Galaxy Tab 2. So how do you search your large list of contacts for a specific contact?

1. Tap Apps on the Home screen.

2. Tap Contacts.

3. Tap the Find Contacts field and use the keyboard to type the name of the contact you are looking for. As soon as you begin to type, the screen displays the contact that most closely reflects what you've typed into the field. Continue typing until you have narrowed the search.

4. View the contact in its entirety by tapping the down arrow in the Notification bar to close the keyboard.

5. Tap the X located in the Search field to clear the Search field of your term. The contact that appears from your search remains visible in the Contacts screen.

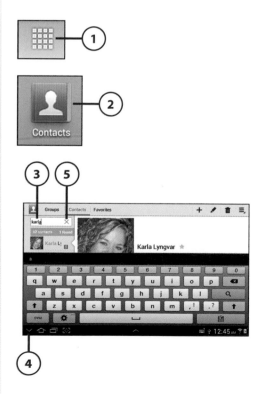

Joining Contacts

When you synchronize the contacts on your Galaxy Tab 2 with multiple accounts, such as Facebook, Twitter, and Google, you can have varying numbers and address information for a single contact. You can see all the contacts' numbers and addresses in a single contact entry by joining contacts. Joining contacts can help you keep your contact information up to date.

1. In the Apps screen, tap Contacts. Your contact information appears on the screen.

2. Scroll down the contact list until you find the contact to which you want to join another contact. Tap and hold your finger on the contact name in the list until a pop-up menu appears.

3. Tap Join Contact in the menu.

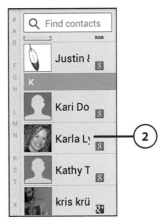

4. In the Join Contact window, scroll down the list until you see the name of the contact you want to join to the contact you selected in Step 2. The contacts are now joined and the information for both entries in each account has merged.

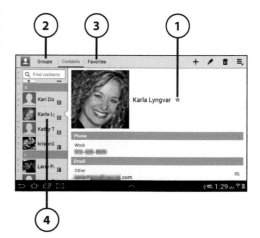

How Do I Unjoin Contacts?

Unjoin contacts by tapping the contact that has the joined contacts attached to it. For example, if Contact A is joined to Contact B, tap Contact A's name in the list. Then tap the Menu icon in the upper-right corner of the screen. In the menu, tap Separate Contact. In the Separate Contact window, tap the minus sign next to Contact B. Tap OK to separate the link. Contact B's information is no longer in the record for Contact A.

Using Contacts

After you have entered a contact in your Galaxy Tab 2, you can utilize a few functions and displays directly from the Contacts page. Start by opening a contact's record.

1. Tap the star icon to the left of the contact name to set that contact as a favorite.

2. Tap the Groups tab to view the list of contacts you have assigned to a group.

3. Tap the Favorites tab to view the list of contacts you have designated as favorites.

4. Tap the Contacts tab, and then press and hold your finger on a contact's name in the contact list.

5. In the contact menu, tap Share Namecard Via.

6. In the Share Namecard Via window, share a namecard via Bluetooth, the ChatON messaging service, the Dropbox web file sharing service, email, Gmail, or Wi-Fi. Think of a namecard as an electronic business card.

Karla Lyngvar
Edit
Delete
Join contact
Remove from favorites
Add to group
Share namecard via ———— ⑤

Share namecard via
Bluetooth
ChatON
Dropbox
Email
Gmail
Wi-Fi Direct ———— ⑥

Managing Contacts

After a contact has been entered into your Galaxy Tab 2, you can manage many of the features of a contact by pressing your finger to a contact and holding. Options include Join Contact, Add to Favorites, Add to Group, Share Namecard Via, and Print Namecard.

7. Compose a new email to your contact by scrolling down the Contact screen until you reach the Email section and then tap the email icon to the right of the contact's email address.

Managing Your Busy Schedule

The S Planner app enables you to manage all your appointments and events from one convenient location. Calendar enables you to view a busy schedule in multiple views such as Day, Week, Month, and List. You can also instruct Calendar to send you a little reminder, in the form of an alert, before an event to help ensure that you never miss a meeting and are always on time.

Creating Calendar Events

Your Galaxy Tab 2 was designed for you to be mobile while still enabling you to manage the important stuff, such as doctor appointments, business meetings, and anniversaries. The S Planner enables you to add important event dates to calendars to help ensure that you do not overlook them.

1. Tap Apps on the Home screen.

2. Swipe the screen from right to left to move to the second page on the Apps screen. Tap S Planner.

3. By default, the calendar opens to the Year view. Tap the Month tab to open the current month. The current date displays a blue circle around the date.

4. Tap the date for which you want to add an event. The date becomes highlighted.

5. Tap the + button at the top-right corner of the screen.

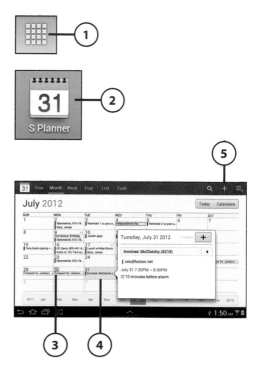

6. The Title field is selected by default. Type a title for the event in the field.

7. Tap the date and time buttons in the From field to enter the start date and time of the event. You can also use the controls in the Set Date window to designate an event for a future date and not just the date you specified in Step 4. When you tap the Date button, a calendar opens, enabling you to select a future date.

8. Tap the controls to enter the start time for the event.

9. Tap Set.

10. Tap the Date tab in the To field to bring up the controls and set the date for the event as you did when you set the date in the From field.

11. Tap the Time tab in the To field to bring up the controls. Adjust the end time for the event in the same manner as setting the begin time.

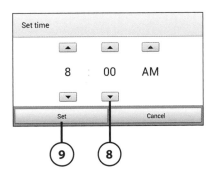

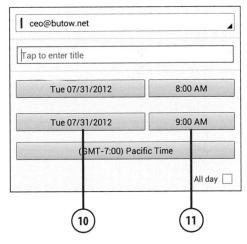

12. Tap the Time Zone button to change the time zone for the event.

13. If the event will happen all day, tap the All Day check box.

14. Tap Repeat if you need to set a repeating cycle for the event. Scroll down to see more options you can set.

15. Tap the Location field to add a location for the event. If you want to find the location in the Maps app, tap the Maps button to the right of the field. You find out more about using the Maps app in Chapter 11, "Using Maps, Navigation, Local, and Latitude."

16. Tap the Description field to type a description for the event.

17. Tap Reminders to choose an alarm time for the event. You can choose the time you want the reminder to either appear as a notification in the Notification bar or you can send the notification to your email account. Tap the plus button at the right of the Reminders field to add another notification that will appear at a different time and/or delivered in a different manner.

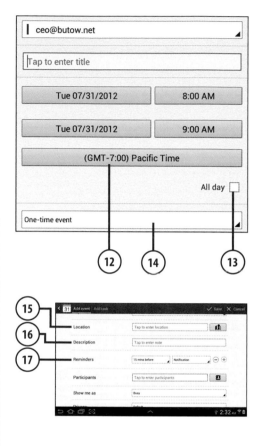

How Do I View the Reminder in the Notification Bar?

When you receive a reminder, you get an audio reminder and also see a reminder icon to the left of the clock in the Notification bar. Tap the clock to open the notification and settings area. The reminder displays at the bottom of the area.

18. Tap the Participants field to add names from your contacts. If you want to select names from the Contacts app, tap the Contact button to the right of the field. In the pop-up window that appears, select one or more contacts by tapping the check box to the left of the contact name.

19. By default, the calendar shows you as busy and blocks out that time so anyone else who views your calendar sees that you're unavailable. Tap the Show Me As field if you want others to see that you're available even during the event. Scroll down to set more options.

20. By default the event is public so anyone who sees your calendar can view it. If you want to make the event private so only you can see it, tap the Privacy field and then tap Private in the menu.

21. If you want to add an image to the event, tap the plus icon to the right of the Images field. You can then take a photo in the Camera app or you can select an image from the Gallery app. You find out how to take photos in Chapter 10, "Capturing and Managing Photos."

22. Tap Save to complete the event and save it to your calendar.

Using Calendar Views

There are six views in which you can view the contents of your calendar: Year, Day, Week, Month, List, and Task. This section examines each view.

Year View

The Year View shows the entire calendar year. At the bottom of the screen, the current year is highlighted at the bottom of the screen. Tap one of the two previous years to the left or the two forthcoming years to the right of the current year to view a calendar for that year. When you change the year, your selected year appears highlighted in the center and links to the two previous years and two subsequent years appear on either side of the selected year.

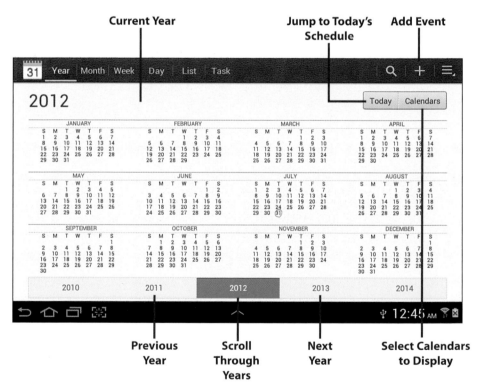

Two buttons appear to the right of the year. Tap Today to highlight the current date in the calendar. Tap Calendars to select the calendars that appear on the screen from all accounts. These accounts include the calendars stored within the app and all web service accounts connected to your system, such as your Google account.

Day View

The Day view is composed of a list of events blocked for each half hour, with a section at the bottom that enables you to scroll through days and jump to the next or previous month.

Jump to | Select
Today's | Calendars
Schedule | to Display | Add Event

| 31 | Year | Month | Week | **Day** | List | Task | | Q | + | ≡ |

Tue, Jul **31** 2012 | Today | Calendars |

July 2012

SUN	MON	TUE	WED	THU	FRI	SAT
1	2	3	4	5	6	7
8	9	10	11	12	13	14
15	16	17	18	19	20	21
22	23	24	25	26	27	28
29	(30)	**31**	1	2	3	4
5	6	7	8	9	10	11

All-day event

No all day events

Event list (1)

1 AM

2 AM

3 AM

4 AM

Invoices: McClatch...
7:30PM – 8:00PM

5 AM

Jun 1 2 3 4 5 6 7 8 9 10 11 12 13 14 15 16 17 18 19 20 21 22 23 24 25 26 27 28 29 30 31 Aug

Ψ 2:42 AM

Jump to | Timeline | Scroll | Jump to | Current | Event
Previous | | Through | Next Month | Month | List
Month | | Days

You can press your finger to the list and flick up or down to scroll through the list. All events scheduled with duration of All Day are located at the very top of the list.

Two buttons appear to the right of the date. Tap Today to open the calendar for the current date. Tap Calendars to select the calendars that appear on the screen from all accounts. These accounts include the calendars stored within the app and all web service accounts connected to your system, such as your Gmail account.

The timeline located at the bottom of the screen enables you to scroll or tap forward or backward through days on the calendar. You can also press your finger to the list and swipe left or right to move backward or forward through the schedule in daily increments. Tap the arrows located at each end of the timeline to jump to the previous or next month. The Today button, located in the upper right, enables you to return to the current day's schedule no matter where you are in the calendar.

You can tap an event in the list to view notes, edit the entry, delete the event, or send it via Bluetooth, messaging, the Dropbox web file storage service, email, or Wi-Fi.

Week View

The week view is arranged into seven day parts, with Sunday, Monday, and Tuesday located on the top and Wednesday, Thursday, Friday, and Saturday on the bottom. The timeline located at the bottom enables you to scroll or tap forward or backward one week at a time, and month abbreviations located at each end let you jump to the previous or next month, such as Sep and Nov if you're looking at a week in October.

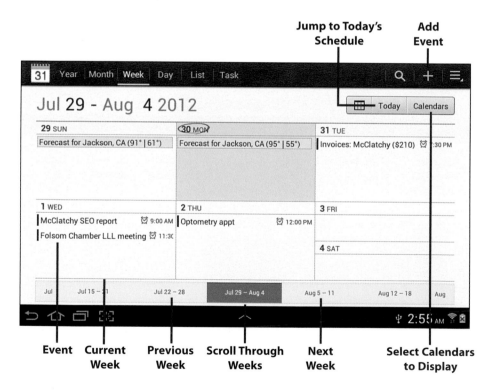

Two buttons appear to the right of the current week. Tap Today to highlight the current date. Tap Calendars to select the calendars that appear on the screen from all accounts. These accounts include the calendars stored within the app and all web service accounts connected to your system, such as your Google account.

Each event for that week is found in its respective scheduled day block. You can tap an event for any date to view notes, edit the entry, delete the event, or send it via Bluetooth, messaging, the Dropbox web file storage service, email, or Wi-Fi.

Month View

The Month view provides a broad view of events for a given month. Month view is composed of two sections: the monthly calendar and the day's event schedule.

Each section lists the events scheduled for that particular month. The current day block you are viewing is highlighted within the calendar section. Any event designated as an All Day Event is highlighted in the day block of the Calendar view.

Two buttons appear to the right of the month. Tap Today to highlight the current date in the calendar. Tap Calendars to select the calendars that appear on the screen from all accounts. These accounts include the calendars stored within the app and all web service accounts connected to your system, such as your Gmail account.

The timeline located at the bottom of the screen becomes a monthly timeline in which you can scroll or tap a new month to view. The arrows located at each end of the timeline enable you to jump to the corresponding month of the previous or next year.

List View

The List view provides a comprehensive view of all scheduled events for an entire year in one list. You can flick the screen upward or downward to view the entire list or use the arrows located at the bottom to jump to a previous year's event schedule or a subsequent year's.

You can tap an event to view notes, edit the entry, delete the event, or send it via Bluetooth, messaging, the Dropbox web file storage service, email, or Wi-Fi.

Task View

The Task View contains the current monthly task and the list of tasks on the right side of the screen. If you don't have any tasks, tap the Tap to add tasks icon in the center of the screen.

1. If you're assigning the task to someone else who also uses S Planner on your Galaxy Tab 2, tap the Task field and select the appropriate person in the menu.

2. The Title field is selected by default. Type a title for the event in the field.

3. Tap the date button in the Due Date field to enter the due date for the task. When you tap the date button, a calendar opens in the Set Date window, enabling you to select a due date.

4. Tap the controls to enter the due date for the event.

5. Tap Set.

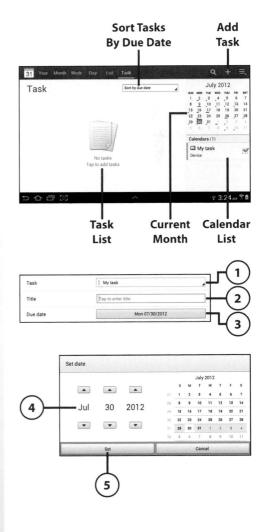

Sort Tasks By Due Date

Add Task

Task List

Current Month

Calendar List

6. If there is no due date, tap the No Due Date check box.

7. By default, there is no reminder for your task. Tap the right arrow button to the right of the Reminder field to open the Reminder window and set a reminder type. You can set a reminder on the due date or set a customized reminder, which is on a date of your choosing.

8. The default priority for the task is Medium. Tap the Priority field to change the priority level in the menu to High, Medium, or Low.

9. If you want to assign the task to a specific group, tap the Group field and select the group from the menu. Scroll down to view more options.

10. Tap the Description field to type a description for the event.

11. If you want to add an image along with the text, tap the plus icon to the right of the Images field. You can then take a photo in the Camera app or you can select an image from the Gallery app. You find out how to take photos in Chapter 10.

12. Tap Save to complete the task and save it to your calendar. The task appears in the Task screen.

Purchase and download music from your Tab

Record video

Play and manage your music

Play and manage your videos

Download and manage podcasts

In this chapter, you find out how to get the most out of the media and entertainment capabilities of the Galaxy Tab. Topics in this chapter include the following:

8

→ Purchasing music, movies, and TV shows
→ Playing videos
→ Recording video
→ Copying files with Windows Media Player
→ Connecting as a mass storage device
→ Using Samsung Kies for PCs and Macs
→ Adding a podcast app
→ Playing songs
→ Creating your own playlists
→ Viewing YouTube videos

Playing Music and Video

Your Galaxy Tab 2 is a digital media player packed with entertainment possibilities as well as a camcorder capable of recording 1080p HD video. You can play music, movies, TV shows, podcasts, audiobooks, and videos; read eBooks; view photos; and access YouTube. Your Tab is preloaded with a variety of apps for purchasing and downloading media.

Purchasing Music, Movies, and TV Shows on Google Play

Google Play makes it easy for you to browse, purchase, and download the latest music, movies, and popular TV shows to your Galaxy Tab 2. To access Google Play for the first time, you must use your Google account to sign in to Google Play. If this is your first time shopping Google Play, you will find the interface very easy to navigate. A great way to become acquainted with Google Play is just to start browsing and previewing music. The process for downloading free content and paid content is similar, but you need to designate a payment method to make purchases.

1. Tap Play Store on the Home screen. If this is your first time launching Google Play, tap Continue and then accept the Terms of Service.

2. Tap the content that you want to purchase. This example uses the Music category.

3. Featured music is listed on the page. Scroll up and down the page to review groups of music.

4. Google Play also makes it possible to browse music by categories such as Top Albums and Genres. Flick the page to explore more categories.

5. If you know the name of the song or album that you want, tap the search icon to specify a search term.

6. Tap a music collection.

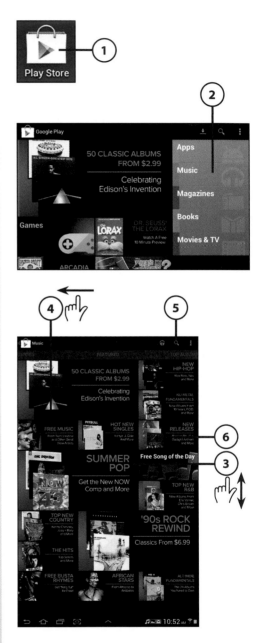

7. Tap an album to go to the description page and read more about the product.

8. Tap to preview a song. If you were browsing movies, there is the option to view trailers.

9. Read reviews at the bottom of the screen.

10. Tap to use the Google Play Music service to play music and other audio files that you have copied from your computer or music store online.

11. Tap to share the music you have found via Google+, email, and more.

12. Tap Menu to access your Google account information, tweak settings, and access online help on how to use Google Play.

13. Tap the price of the album or a song to enter your payment information and then make the purchase.

>>>Go Further

GOOGLE PLAY MUSIC

Google Play Music is a service that enables you to access your personal music collection online, wireless and without syncing. You can take advantage of this service on other compatible Android devices as well. Instantly play the music you have purchased on Google Play and you can upload up to 20,000 songs. You can find the Google Play Music app in the Apps menu.

>>>Go Further

SAMSUNG MEDIA HUB

The Samsung Media Hub app preinstalled on your Galaxy Tab 2 is another portal to hundreds of movies and TV shows available for you to rent or purchase. You must create a Media Hub account before you can begin to purchase your favorite movies and TV shows.

Playing Videos

The 10.1" high-resolution screen of your Galaxy Tab 2 provides a great outlet for viewing your favorite videos. The Video shortcut on your Galaxy Tab 2 was designed to make it easy for you to browse and play your downloaded and recorded videos.

1. Tap the Apps icon from a Home screen.

2. Tap the Apps category, flick to the left to view the second Apps screen page, and then tap Video Player to access your video libraries.

3. Videos are arranged in ways: thumbnail images of your videos, a list view of videos on your Tab, videos grouped by folder, and video shared from other devices. Tap a category to view a list of videos.

4. Tap a video in the list to begin playing it.

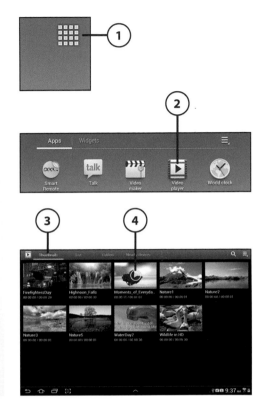

OTHER VIDEO OPTIONS

Tap the Menu button to choose how videos are listed, shared, and deleted or to customize playback options. The Menu button is located in the upper-right corner of the interface. The List By options enable you to arrange a video library by Name, Date, Size, and Type. The Share Via option enables you to upload videos to YouTube, Google+, AllShare, Bluetooth, Wi-Fi Direct, Dropbox, and even Gmail. The Auto Play Next feature is set to Off by default, but you can configure your Galaxy Tab 2 to automatically begin playing the next video in the list after the current video ends. You also can touch and hold your finger on a video in the list to reveal contextual menu options, such as Share Via, Delete, and Details.

5. After the video has started, tap in the middle of the screen to bring up the playback controls.

6. Slide your finger on the Volume slider to adjust the volume of the video.

7. Tap the Screen View icon to change the display mode to full screen or to return to the normal view.

8. Tap the speaker icon to mute the sound. Tap again to unmute.

9. Tap the SoundAlive icon to set the sound quality to Normal, Voice, Movie, or Virtual 7.1 ch.

10. Drag your finger across the Movie Timeline to advance through the video or jump to a new location. You can also tap the timeline in a new location to jump to that location.

11. The Play button, located in the Playback controls, turns into a Pause button as the video plays. Tap the Pause button to pause the video.

12. Tap the Forward or Rewind buttons to move forward or backward through the video.

13. Tap the Bookmarks icon to mark points in the video that you can revisit later.

14. Tap the Menu button.

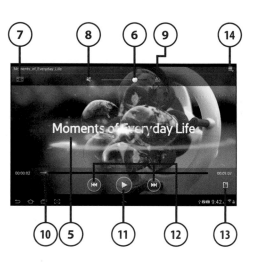

15. Tap Share Via to share the video using ChatON, Dropbox, Google+, Bluetooth, Wi-Fi Direct, YouTube, Gmail, or Email.

16. Tap to edit the beginning and end of a video by performing a trim.

17. Tap to share the video with other devices via Bluetooth.

18. Tap to open this video in the Video Maker app to perform basic edits and create a new video.

19. Tap to configure play speed, subtitles, and auto play settings.

20. Tap to view details of the video such as Name, Size, Resolution, Duration, Format, and sDate Modified.

21. Tap to set the app to automatically turn off video after playing a certain amount of time. Options include After 15 min, After 30 min, After 1 hr, After 1 hr 30 min, or After 2 hr.

22. Tap to connect to nearby devices. You learn how to use Bluetooth devices with your Galaxy Tab 2 in the "Pairing Bluetooth Devices" section of Chapter 13, "Adding New Hardware."

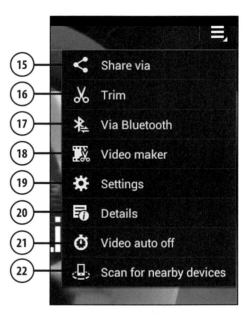

Recording Video

Your Galaxy Tab 2 is capable of recording 1080p HD video with its main 3-megapixel camera located on the rear of the device. The Galaxy Tab 2 is also equipped with some very helpful features commonly found on dedicated camcorders, including white balance, a video light, manual exposure, and effects.

1. Tap the Camera icon to access the camera feature. Tap OK if any camera tips display.

2. Move the mode button into the camcorder position to record video. Your Galaxy Tab 2 switches to video mode.

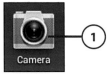

Options Under Settings

Some of the settings located under the Settings icon are the same setting represented as separate icons in the Camera interface. For example, the Effect option in the Settings menu includes the same options you find if you tap of the magic wand icon. The next few steps cover settings options that are unique to the Settings menu. Anything omitted in the Settings menu is covered under its respective icon on the interface.

Order of Menu Options Differs

If you are using the 7.0 Tab, it is important to note that the order within the Settings menu is slightly different.

3. Tap the Settings icon to customize Camera settings.

4. Tap Edit Shortcuts to customize the first five shortcuts to camera settings in the settings menu: Self-Recording, Recording Mode, Exposure Value, Timer, and Effects. You can swap out these settings with others that appear when you tap Edit Shortcuts. Just drag a new setting on top of an old one to replace it.

5. Tap Resolution to set a size for the images you capture.

6. Tap to choose an automatic white balance for the camera. The white balance features help accurately reproduce colors when you are recording in various lighting situations so that neutral colors, such as white and gray, are truly neutral and all colors are rendered without undesired color casts.

7. Scroll further down the menu to reveal more options.

8. Tap to enable or disable an onscreen grid that can help you with composition of the photo.

9. Tap Storage to determine whether the photos you capture are stored on an optional memory card or on your Tab.

10. Tap to return the Camera settings to the default settings.

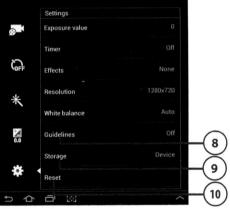

11. An image that is too light or too dark degrades the appearance of your photos. To take full advantage of the camera feature of the Galaxy Tab, you must adjust the exposure level for various bright or dark lighting conditions. Tap the Exposure Value icon.

12. Drag the exposure level up to achieve a proper exposure level in a low-light shooting environment, or drag it down for a very bright shooting environment.

13. Tap the Effects icon to add camera effects to your videos as you capture them. Your choices are Negative, Black and White, and Sepia.

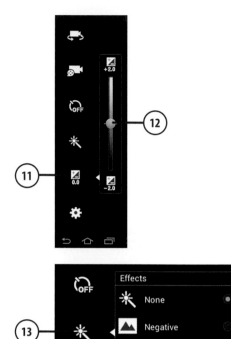

Adding Camera Effects

Keep in mind that when you use any of the video effects, such as Negative, Black and White, and Sepia, they become a permanent part of your videos. To give yourself more choices in the future as to how you use your images, consider purchasing a video-editing program that enables you to perform such effects but still maintain your original video.

14. Tap the Timer icon to designate how long the Tab should wait before the camera starts to record. This is great for allowing you time to set up the shot and then place yourself in the frame.

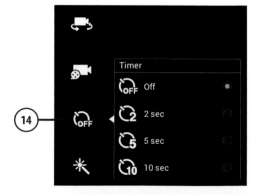

15. Tap the Recording mode icon to optimize your video for being sent as an email attachment and limit the size of the video you record to 50 megabytes.

16. Tap to switch between the rear-facing and front-facing cameras.

17. Compose the scene in the Viewer.

18. Tap the Record button to begin recording.

19. The Record button turns into a Stop button after you begin recording. Tap the Stop button to end recording.

20. The video you just recorded appears in the Image Viewer. Tap the Image Viewer to review the recorded video.

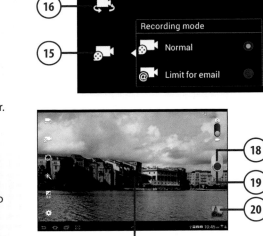

Copying Files with Windows Media Player

When you connect your Galaxy Tab 2 to your PC with the data cable, you can choose how you want to connect and/or synchronize media files with your Galaxy Tab. One option is to sync your computer and your Galaxy Tab 2 with Windows Media Player. Follow these steps to copy music and movies to your Galaxy Tab 2.

1. Connect the data cable from the Galaxy Tab to the USB port on your computer.

2. In the AutoPlay window on your PC, click Sync Digital Media Files to This Device using Windows Media Player.

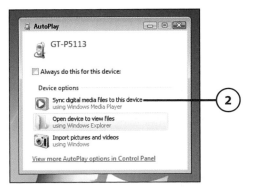

3. Windows Media Player opens and lists media items available for you to copy to the Tab.

4. Click and drag the item(s) you want to copy to the Sync list.

5. The list of music you select appears in the Sync list. All tracks in the albums are selected by default. You can deselect any songs that you do not want to copy by right-clicking the song and clicking Remove from List.

6. Tap Start Sync to begin copying the files from your PC to your Galaxy Tab.

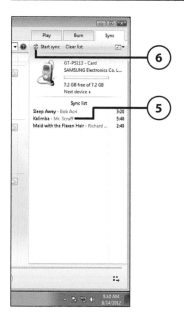

7. After sync is complete, the music is available for playback by tapping the Music Player app on your Tab.

Connecting as a Mass Storage Device

You can drag and drop files from a PC to your Galaxy Tab 2 by connecting as a removable disk. Follow these steps to transfer music from your PC to your Galaxy Tab 2 using the Mass Storage USB mode.

1. Connect the data cable to the Galaxy Tab 2 and the USB connector to the USB port on your computer.

2. In the AutoPlay window on your computer, click Open Device to View Files using Windows Explorer to drag and drop music files directly from your computer into a folder on your Galaxy Tab 2.

3. Your Tab appears as a removable disk in the Computer section.

4. Display the home Tablet directory by double-clicking the removable disk in the folder tree.

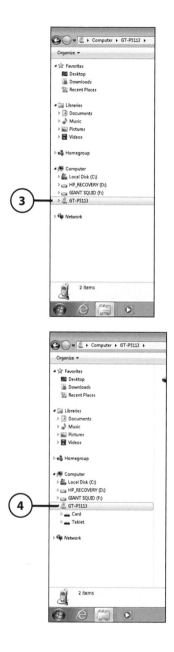

5. Display the Tablet folders by double-clicking Tablet.

6. If you do not already have a media folder, create a new folder on your Tab.

7. Locate the files that you want to transfer onto your computer and then drag them to the Music folder on your Tab. The files are copied to your device.

8. After you have finished copying files to your Tab from your computer, remove the USB cable from the PC.

9. When you tap the Music Player shortcut on your Tab, the music you have transferred is available for playback.

⑤   ⑦

>>>Go Further

CONNECTING TO A MAC

You need extra software to connect your Tab to a Mac. Android File Transfer is an application for Macs running OS X 10.5 or later that enables you to view and transfer files between your Mac and Galaxy Tab 2. This application works with Android devices running Android 3.0 or later. You can download Android File Transfer from http://www.android.com/filetransfer/.

Samsung Kies for PCs and Macs

The Samsung Kies application makes it easy for you to manage your music, movies, and photos between your computer and your Galaxy Tab 2. When you connect your Tab to your PC or Mac, Samsung Kies acts much like iTunes and Windows Media Player, enabling you to sync your content libraries.

PC and Mac Interfaces

The Multimedia Sync interface is slightly different in PC and Mac versions. You can perform these first few steps on either version, regardless of a few interface differences. The following steps are demonstrated on a PC.

1. After you have installed Samsung Kies onto your computer, connect your Tab to your PC or Mac. Close the AutoPlay window that pops up on your PC.

2. Launch Samsung Kies on your computer. Your Tab opens under the Connected devices list in the sidebar on the left side of the interface.

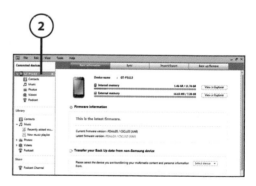

3. If this is your first time using Samsung Kies, you need to populate the library with music located on your computer. Click Music under Library.

4. Click Add Music Folder.

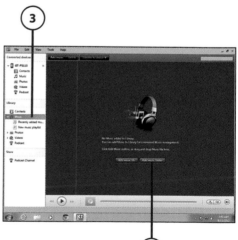

5. Click Music.

6. Select the Music folder(s) that you want to import.

7. Click Select Folder to import the music into your Samsung Kies library. You can drag files from the Music library and drop them directly onto your Tab under Connected devices.

8. Select your Tab under Connected Devices.

9. Click Sync.

10. Select the content that you want to sync to your Tab. As soon as you click the check box for a multimedia category, you are able to select all content for that category or select only specific content.

11. Click Sync. The content is synced to your Tab.

It's Not All Good

USAGE RESTRICTIONS

Some of the music in your Library is Digital Rights Management (DRM) protected, which means use of those files has been restricted. These music files are from a time when music was not DRM free on iTunes. You won't be able to transfer these songs without upgrading them for a fee. Visit the iTunes Store for more information.

Adding a Podcast App

One popular podcast manager is BeyondPod and the lite version is free. The lite version has all of the features of the Pro version except scheduling of updates is disabled, you can update only one feed at a time, and you can download only one podcast at a time. If you want all the bells and whistles BeyondPod has to offer, you can purchase an unlock key for $6.99.

1. After you have installed the BeyondPod app, tap to launch the app.

2. In the All Feeds screen, tap a podcast to view the episodes.

3. Tap to download the RSS feed.

4. Tap to view episode notes.

5. Tap to add or remove an episode from the playlist.

6. Tap an episode to play it. The episode immediately begins to play.

7. Use the Playback controls to pause or jump forward or backward in the video. Use the slider to shuttle through the video.

8. Tap back twice to get back to the All Feeds page.

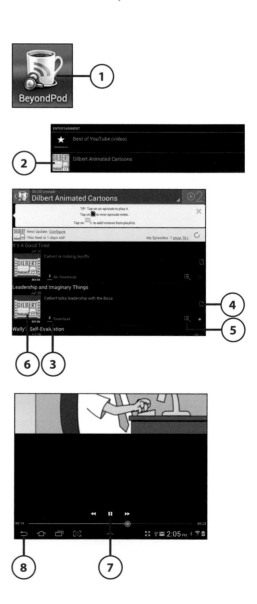

9. Tap Episodes to view all of the video and audio podcasts you have played. When you tap through to the All Episodes page, you can further filter with results show on this page in the bottom-left corner of the screen. You can filter by Audio Only, Video Only, Downloaded, Unfinished, and Locked.

10. Tap to play the current podcast in the playlist.

11. Tap to filter which feeds show on this page and manage feed categories.

12. Hold your finger to a feed to update, delete, edit, or share that feed with someone else.

13. Tap to refresh all feeds on the page.

14. Tap to browse other popular feeds and add new feeds to the page.

15. Tap the menu for more options and receive support for the app.

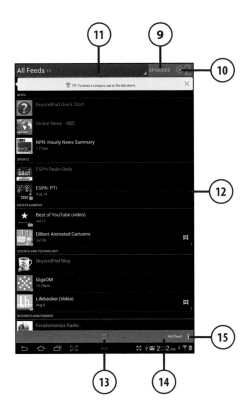

Automatically Updating Feeds

By default, feeds are set to automatically update on a configurable interval. You can change the interval by tapping Menu in the status bar, tapping More, tapping Settings, and then tapping Feed Update Settings to change the interval.

Deleting Feeds

If you want to delete a feed, tap and hold your finger to a downloaded feed. A pop-up menu displays that includes a Delete Feed option.

Playing Songs

The Music Player on your Galaxy Tab 2 was designed to make it easy for you to browse and play your music collection. A great set of headphones can enhance the enjoyment of your favorite music. The ability to browse your Tab's music library and understanding your playback options are a big step toward getting the most out of your Tab's many entertainment possibilities.

1. Tap the Apps icon from a Home screen.

2. Tap Apps.

3. Tap Music Player. Music Player automatically shows a list of songs on your Tab.

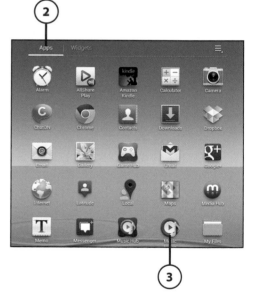

4. Tap the menu to delete a song, share a song, set an alarm tone, scan for nearby devices, or access more Music Player settings.

5. Tap to create a new playlist.

6. Tap to search the Music Player library.

7. Tap the appropriate category to filter the music in the Music Player library.

8. Tap a song to play it. The playback controls automatically appear at the bottom of the screen.

9. Tap the cover of the song that is currently playing to open it full screen.

10. Tap the star to mark a track as favorite.

11. Tap to mute the volume.

12. Drag to adjust the volume.

13. Tap the SoundAlive icon to add an equalizer effect such as Pop, Rock, Dance, and more.

14. Tap to view information about the current album.

15. Tap to view a list of all songs in Music Player.

16. Tap the Menu to add a song to a playlist, share a song with another device, use a song to set an alarm tone, scan for nearby devices, save a playlist, and access more Music Player settings.

17. Flick the screen to the left to go to the next song.

18. Tap to enable or disable shuffling during playback.

19. Tap to enable or disable looping of a song or album.

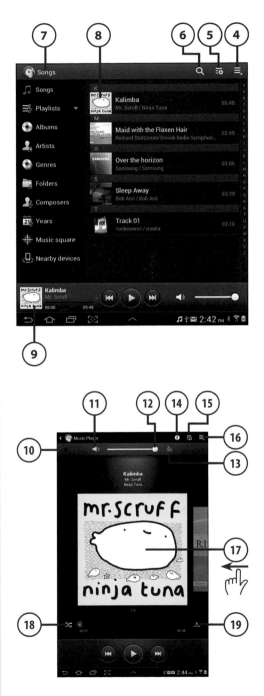

Creating Your Own Playlists

Playlists are a great way to create a compilation of your favorite songs for playback on your Galaxy Tab 2. Use playlists as an opportunity to organize the best songs from your favorite artists, acoustic selections, party music, classic rock, orchestral masterpieces, relaxation tracks, and more.

1. Tap the Music Player shortcut on your Tab.

2. Tap the Playlists icon.

3. Tap New Playlist.

4. Type the name for your new playlist.

5. Tap OK. A green plus sign appears next to songs.

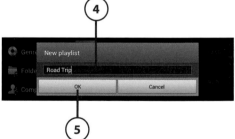

6. Tap the songs that you want to appear in the playlist.

7. The songs you choose appear at the bottom within the Playlist.

8. If you change your mind about a song, tap the minus sign to delete it from the playlist.

9. Tap Done when you are finished creating the playlist. You can also cancel the playlist.

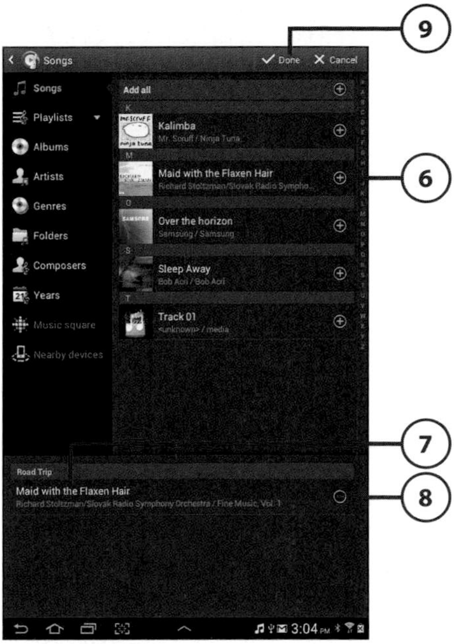

REMOVING AND ADDING SONGS IN A PLAYLIST

You can remove songs from a playlist by selecting the playlist and then tapping Delete in the application menu at the top of the screen. Select the track(s) you want to remove by tapping the check box next each item and then tap Remove. You can add a song to a playlist by opening the playlist to which you want to add the song and then tapping the Add Music icon in the application bar. You can then select additional music from the library.

Viewing YouTube Videos

The high-resolution screen of the Galaxy Tab 2, along with its portability and built-in video camera, makes it great for viewing and sharing videos online. The preinstalled YouTube widget gives you the capability to browse and view videos posted by users from around the world. You can also upload videos as soon as you shoot them with your Tab.

1. Tap YouTube on the default Home screen. A list of featured videos displays.

2. Flick the screen to see many more video selections.

3. Tap Browse to view the many video categories of YouTube.

4. Tap Account to designate your YouTube account information.

5. Tap to search for a YouTube video.

6. Tap to sign in to your YouTube account, access more YouTube settings, read online Help documentation, and send feedback about the app.

7. Tap a video to play it.

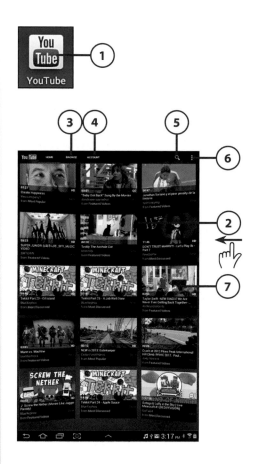

8. Tap to bookmark a video, add to Favorites, and create a new playlist.

9. Tap to share the current video via Wi-Fi Direct, ChatON, Google+, Bluetooth, Dropbox, or email.

Other Sharing Options

Other sharing options might appear in this list if you have downloaded apps that allow for additional sharing features, such as BeyondPod.

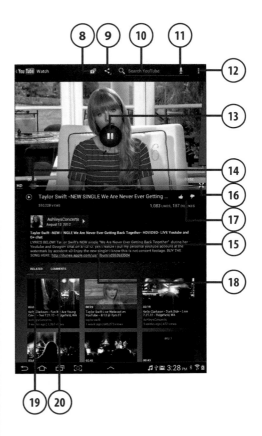

10. Tap to search YouTube for a new video.

11. Tap to speak a search for a new video.

12. Tap to set up your Tab so that you can watch YouTube on a compatible TV, copy the URL of the current video, flag a video, access more YouTube settings, get help, and send feedback to the app developer.

13. Tap to pause and play the current video.

14. Drag to move through the current video.

15. Tap to visit the channel of the user who posted this video.

16. Tap to play the video full screen.

17. Tap to rate the video by giving it a thumbs up or thumbs down.

18. Read the video description.

19. Tap to view videos that are similar to this one.

20. Tap to read comments about this video from other users and to create a response of your own.

Purchase and read newspapers, books, and magazines with Readers Hub

Readers Hub

Daily News
NEW EXPERIENCE

News
Powered by
PressDisplay

Book

Books
Powered by
Kobo

MAGAZINE
October 2010

Update
Magazines
Powered by
Zinio

8:49 AM

SAMSUNG

Find out how to purchase newspapers, books, and magazines using Readers Hub and how to read them on your Galaxy Tab 2. Topics in this chapter include:

→ Logging in to your account

→ Purchasing books

→ Using reading aids

→ Adding bookmarks, highlights, and notes

→ Organizing your books

Reading and Managing Books

Your Galaxy Tab 2 offers a great outlet for you to enjoy books. The Readers Hub app that is installed on your Tab offers a stylish eReader that enables you to browse, purchase, download, and read newspapers, eBooks, and magazines from your device. The Galaxy Tab 2 also comes loaded with the Play Books app (including three free books) and the Amazon Kindle app.

Both the Play Books and Amazon Kindle apps enable you to enhance your reading experience by offering reading aids such as the ability to increase font size and change background color, which are features also included in Readers Hub. If you prefer a different eReader, you can shop Google Play for other apps and then download and add books from other sources. Consider trying out a few of the available readers to see which one you like the best.

Logging In to Your Account

Logging In to Your PressDisplay Account

The News, Books, and Magazine sections of Readers Hub each have their own registration process. Before you can begin purchasing content, you must first set up an account. When you tap the Readers Hub app on the Home screen for the first time, a disclaimer opens. Follow these directions to set up an account to subscribe to newspapers.

1. Tap the Readers Hub icon to launch the application.

2. Read the Disclaimer and then tap Confirm.

3. Tap News. A notice appears informing you that you can download seven trial newspapers. If this notice appears, just tap the screen to accept.

4. Your recently downloaded newspapers appear in your Library. Tap the settings icon in the upper-right corner of the screen.

5. Tap Accounts.

6. Tap Register.

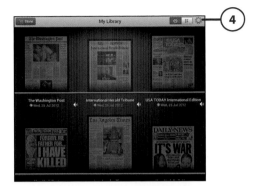

7. Tap the registration option you would like to have, and then follow the prompts to set up the account.

Logging In to Your Kobo Account

Before you can begin purchasing books, you must first set up a Kobo account. Follow these directions to set up your Kobo account. These directions assume that you have already launched the Readers Hub app.

1. Tap Books. The Terms of Use display.

2. Read the Terms of Use and then tap Agree.

3. Tap Sign In.

4. Tap Create to register as a new customer.

5. Fill in the account fields. If you want, you can deselect the Yes, Send Me Newsletters, Coupons and Special Offers from Kobo via Email field.

6. Tap Create Account when you are finished.

7. Decide whether you want the browser to remember this password.

Talking About Security

If you are not the only user of your Galaxy Tab 2, you might want to consider choosing Not Now or Never on the Confirm screen so that you have some level of security to prevent unauthorized purchases.

8. Now you are ready to shop.

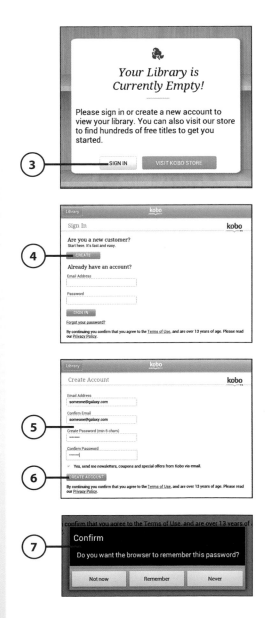

Purchasing Books

You can find many free books in the Kobo library, and purchasing a book is easy. After you find a book that you want to purchase, Kobo simply walks you through process of entering your billing information. Follow these steps to purchase books using your Kobo account.

1. Tap Books. Your library opens.

2. Tap Store to begin browsing for books to purchase.

3. Find a book that you want to purchase and then tap the book. The synopsis page opens for the book.

4. Tap Buy Now. The Checkout page opens.

5. Enter your Payment Method information into the fields. A tip screen for keyboard gestures might appear when you first tap in a field. If it does appear, you can choose the option to not show the tip screen again and then tap OK to make the screen go away.

6. Scroll down and enter your Billing Address information.

7. Scroll down and enter Promo Code and (or) Gift Card information.

8. Tap Buy Now to complete the transaction.

9. Tap Update Library. The book downloads to your library.

Changing Account Settings

If you need to edit information in your Kobo account, such as adding a new credit card or editing a shipping address, you can tap Buy Now for a book you want to purchase and then choose Change Details. Kobo remembers your checkout information after you have made a purchase.

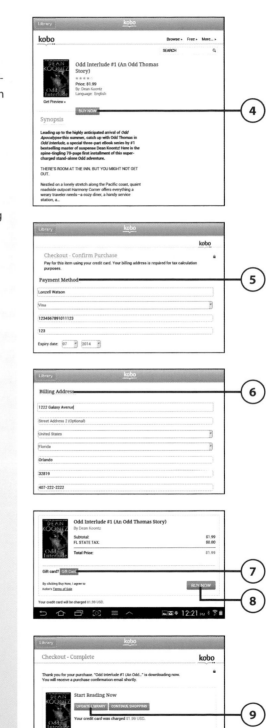

Using Reading Aids

Your Galaxy Tab contains many options for enhancing your eBook experience, including changing background color, font size, jumping to locations within the book, and organizing your book titles.

1. Tap the book you want to read from your library. Reading Tips appear. Tap Dismiss to skip the tips for now.

2. Tap Start Reading. The cover page opens.

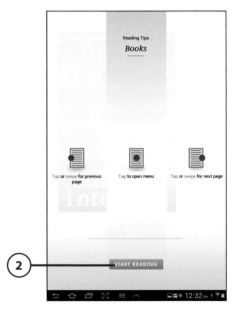

3. Tap the right side of the book page to progress to the next page. Tap the left side of the page to revisit the previous page. You can also flick left or right to turn pages.

4. Go to a page with text and then tap the middle of the screen to access reading aid controls.

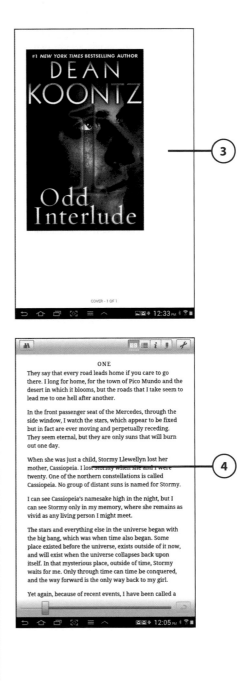

5. Tap to access the table of contents for the book. You can jump to a chapter by tapping its title in the contents.

6. Tap the info icon to read an overview of the book.

Contents

Cover	>
Title Page	>
Copyright	>
Contents	>
Part One: South of Moonlight Bay	>
✓ Chapter One	>
Chapter Two	>
Chapter Three	>
Chapter Four	>
Chapter Five	>
Chapter Six	>
Chapter Seven	>
TO BE CONTINUED in Odd	>

Overview

★★★★☆

Odd Interlude #1
by Dean Koontz
Random House Publishing Group

f SHARE

Leading up to the highly anticipated arrival of *Odd Apocalypse* this summer, catch up with Odd Thomas in *Odd Interlude*, a special three-part eBook series by #1 bestselling master of suspense Dean Koontz! Here is the spine-tingling 70-page first installment of this supercharged stand-alone Odd adventure.

THERE'S ROOM AT THE INN. BUT YOU MIGHT NOT GET OUT.

Nestled on a lonely stretch along the Pacific coast, quaint roadside outpost Harmony Corner offers everything a weary traveler needs—a cozy diner, a handy service station, a cluster of motel rooms . . . and the Harmony family homestead presiding over it all. But when Odd Thomas and company stop to spend the night, they discover that there's more to this secluded haven than meets the eye—and that between life and death, there is something more frightening than either.

Includes a preview of the next thrilling novel in Dean Koontz's acclaimed Odd Thomas series: *Odd Apocalypse!*

"Koontz gives his character wit, good humor, a familiarity with the dark side of humanity—and moral outrage."—*USA Today*

"The nice young fry cook with the occult powers is

7. Tap to access any highlighted text and notes you have made in this book. At the bottom of the page, you can view a list of highlights or notes you have made.

8. Tap Reading Settings to change the font size, font style, the page transition effect, and book layout (two pages or single page).

9. Tap to return to your book library.

10. Tap to read the current book.

11. Drag the slider to jump to different pages in the book.

12. After you drag the slider to jump to a different location, you can tap the backward arrow to jump back to where you were last reading.

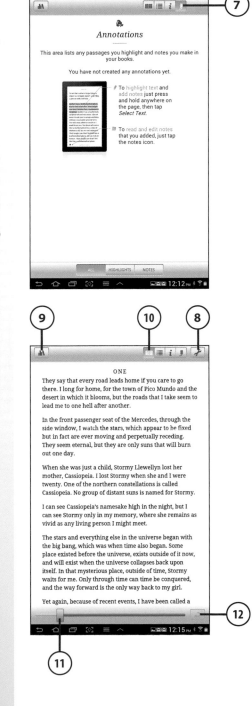

13. Tap the Menu icon at the bottom of the screen to access more options.

14. Tap to select text on a page for highlighting, creating a note, or sharing on Facebook. This is not the only way to select text. You can also hold your finger anywhere on screen to select text. (Read more about highlighting text in the "Adding Bookmarks, Highlights, and Notes" section.)

15. Tap to change the overall font size for the book. Your choices are Smallest, Smaller, Normal, Larger, and Largest.

16. Tap to change the overall font style for the book. Your choices are Serif and System Default.

17. Tap Reading Settings to change font size using a slider, font style, the page transition effect, and the book layout (two pages or single page).

18. Tap to share book passages on your Facebook account.

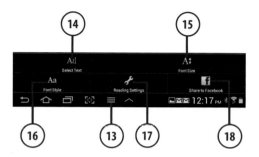

Adding Bookmarks, Highlights, and Notes

Your eBook reader provides the convenience of placing a bookmark where you stopped reading so you can begin at the right location later. You also have the capability to highlight text in a book and to leave notes.

1. When you close a book, a bookmark is automatically placed on the page where you stopped reading. When you open the book again, the book opens to the bookmarked page.

2. You might want to specify a block of text in a block as a point of interest by highlighting it. Press your finger on the screen and hold. An overlay appears giving you the option to Select Text.

3. Tap Select Text. Arrows appear.

4. Drag the handles of the arrows to specify the text you want to highlight.

5. Tap Highlight.

Removing Highlights from Text

You can remove the highlight from text by pressing your finger to the highlighted text. A menu appears giving you the option to delete the text. Tap Delete Highlight.

6. You can leave a note for an excerpt of text. Press your finger on the screen and hold. An overlay appears giving you the option to Select Text.

7. Tap Select Text.

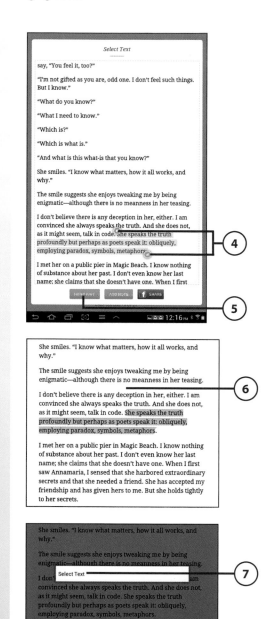

8. Drag the arrows to specify the text for which you want to leave a comment.

9. Tap Add Note. A note field and the keyboard display. If a tip screen opens, just tap OK to make it disappear.

10. Type the note.

11. Tap Save. The passage of text is highlighted and an icon of a note sheet appears at the bottom of the screen.

Deleting a Note

To modify or delete a note, you can tap the icon of a note sheet that appears at the bottom of the screen to reveal the notes on that page. You can then edit your notes or tap an X to delete them.

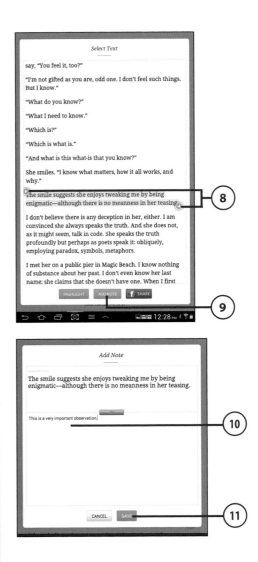

VIEWING ALL NOTES AND MARKS

Your Galaxy Tab 2 offers a quick and convenient way to view and jump to all notes and highlights you have made in a book. Tap the middle of the screen to reveal the book options. You can then tap the icon that looks like a pencil at the top of the screen. From the Annotations screen you can view all of your highlights and notes.

Organizing Your Books

After you have accumulated many titles in your eBook library, you need a method to the madness of organizing your books. By default, your books are ordered by the most recently downloaded on the Kobo home page. You have a couple other sorting options to choose from.

1. From your book library, tap the Menu icon at the bottom of the screen.

2. Tap Sort By to choose from the sorting options.

3. Tap Account to access and edit your Kobo account details.

4. Tap Refresh to update your library with all of your latest, purchased content.

5. Tap Import Content to have Kobo search your memory card for content that can be imported into your library. You have the option of selecting all or some of the files for import.

6. Tap to arrange books in your library into a list.

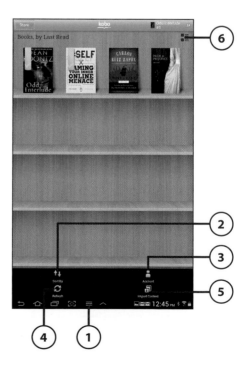

REMOVING AND ARCHIVING BOOKS

>>>Go Further

You can access the option to remove books from your device by pressing your finger down on a book cover in your library. A menu opens from which you can choose the Remove Item option. The book is removed from the library page, but remains archived in your Kobo account.

Browse, manage,
and share photos   Capture photos

Capture a screenshot

In this chapter, you find out how to capture photos and screenshots, share photos via email and slideshows, and view and manage photos with Gallery:

→ Using the camera

→ Navigating Image Viewer

→ Tips for capturing photos

→ Working with Gallery

→ Performing screen captures

→ Editing images

Capturing and Managing Photos

Along with transferring images from other sources, such as your computer or micro SD card, to your Galaxy Tab 2, your Tab is capable of taking high-quality photos and can house thousands of photos organized in categories. You also have the capability to take screenshots of the Tab's interface.

Your Galaxy Tab's high-resolution screen offers a great way to showcase photos to friends and family, but you don't have to stop there. You can also use Photo Editor and Photo Studio, all accessible from Gallery, to perform basic photo edits and even share pictures via AllShare, Bluetooth, Gmail, Messaging, Picasa, and more.

Using the Camera

Your Galaxy Tab 2 uses a 3.0 megapixel rear-facing camera located on the back of the device to take photos, along with a 2.0 megapixel front-facing camera that you can use for self-portraits. Taking a photo can be as simple as choosing a subject, composing your shot, and pressing a button. The Galaxy Tab 2 is also equipped with some helpful features commonly found on dedicated photo cameras, including shooting modes, scene modes, manual exposure, white balance, flash, manual exposure, and ISO settings.

Adjusting Settings and Taking Photos

The Camera application for the Galaxy Tab 2 is chock full of features that can help you capture high-quality images. The interface is simplistic and intuitive.

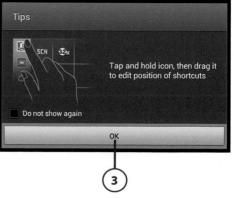

1. Tap the Camera icon to access the camera feature.

2. If you have a micro SD card inserted, you can either tap OK to change the storage settings to the SD Card or tap Cancel to use your Tab's storage to store photos and videos.

3. You can select Do Not Show Again to stop receiving tips on how to use Camera and then tap OK, or you can just tap OK to continue receiving Camera tips.

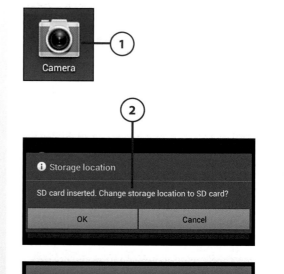

Order of Menu Options Differs

If you are using the 7.0 Tab, it is important to note that the order within the Settings menu is slightly different.

4. Move the mode button into the still image position to capture photos. Still Image mode is the default mode.

5. Tap the Settings icon to customize camera settings.

Options Under Settings

The settings located under the Settings icon are mostly the same setting represented as separate icons in the Camera interface. For example, the Effect option in the Settings menu includes the same options you find if you tap the magic wand icon. The next few steps cover settings options that are unique to the Settings menu. Anything omitted in the Settings menu is covered under its respective icon on the interface.

6. Tap Edit Shortcuts to customize the first five shortcuts to camera settings in the settings menu: Self-Portrait, Shooting Mode, Timer, Exposure Value, and Effects. You can swap out these settings with others that appear when you tap Edit Shortcuts. Just drag a new setting on top of an old one to replace it.

7. Tap to choose an automatic scene mode. Automatic scene modes offer quick and easy ways to adapt to various lighting conditions when taking photos.

8. Tap Resolution to set a size for the images you capture.

9. Scroll further down the menu to reveal more options.

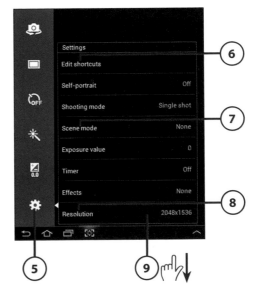

EXPLORING SCENE MODES

The scene mode options optimize your camera for special shooting situations. For example, Landscape mode uses the smallest possible aperture setting for the greatest depth of field to help ensure that everything in a wide vista is in sharp focus.

Night mode uses a flash in combination with a slow shutter speed to brighten dark backgrounds. Sports mode uses a fast shutter speed to capture moving subjects without blurring.

10. Tap to adjust the white balance for the camera. The white balance features help accurately reproduce colors when you are shooting in various lighting situations so that neutral colors, such as white and gray, are truly neutral and all colors are rendered without undesired color casts.

11. Tap to set how the camera measures or meters the light source. This setting determines how the camera factors light in a scene to achieve the proper exposure.

12. Tap to enable or disable an onscreen grid that can help you with composition.

13. Tap to enable or disable GPS tagging of the photos you capture. Embedded GPS information can come in handy if you use a photo-editing and managing application such as iPhoto 9 and later, which enables you to use the location information to manage and showcase photos.

>>>Go Further

TALKING ABOUT CENTRE-WEIGHTED AND SPOT METERING

The default Metering setting is Centre-Weighted. Your other choices are Matrix, which measures light intensity in several points to achieve the best exposure, and Spot, where only a small area in the scene is measured. Matrix metering is usually considered the most accurate form of metering because it measures the entire scene and then sets the exposure according to an average. Spot measuring is generally used to capture very high contrast scenes, such as when a subject's back is to the sun.

14. Tap Storage to determine whether the photos you capture are stored on an optional memory card or on your Tab.

15. Tap to reset the Camera settings to the default settings.

16. An image that is too light or too dark degrades the appearance of your photos. To take full advantage of the camera feature of the Galaxy Tab, you must adjust the exposure level for various bright or dark lighting conditions. Tap the Exposure Value icon.

17. Drag the exposure level up to achieve a proper exposure level in a low-light shooting environment, or drag it down for a very bright shooting environment.

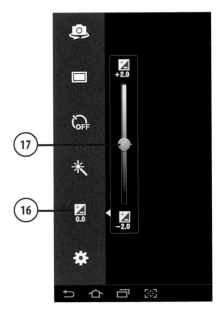

18. Tap to add in camera effects to your photos as you capture them. Your choices are Negative, Black and White, and Sepia.

Adding Camera Effects

Keep in mind that when you use any of the photo effects, such as Negative, Black and White, and Sepia, they become a permanent part of your pictures. To give yourself more choices in the future as to how you use your images, consider purchasing a photo-editing program that enables you to perform such effects but still maintain your original photo.

19. Tap the Timer icon to designate how long the Tab should wait before the camera takes a picture. This is great for allowing you time to set up the shot and then place yourself in the frame.

20. Tap the Shooting mode icon to select a shooting mode. The Galaxy Tab is set to Single Shot by default.

21. Tap to switch between the rear-facing and front-facing cameras.

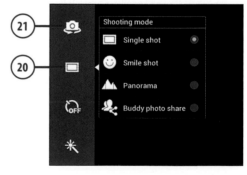

>>>Go Further

EXPLORING SHOOTING MODES

Choose Smile Shot mode to focus the camera on the face of your subject. After the camera detects the person's smile, it takes the picture.

Panorama mode enables you to take a picture and then use the onscreen guide to move the viewfinder and take seven more shots. This is a great mode for capturing wide vistas, such as landscapes and cityscapes.

Select Buddy Photo Share to capture and share photos with your friends using face detection.

22. Compose the subject in the Viewer. By default, Camera automatically focuses on what is in the center of the Viewer.

23. Hold your finger on the Camera button, level the shot, and then remove your finger from the button to capture the image. A thumbnail of the image appears in the Image Viewer.

24. Tap the Image Viewer to review the image you just captured. You can also access your photos by tapping the Gallery icon under Applications from any Home screen.

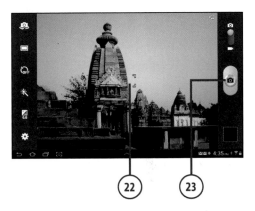

Navigating Image Viewer

Image Viewer provides a quick-and-easy way to review the photos that you have just taken. It also enables you to quickly share your pictures as soon as you capture them or set them as wallpaper. You can also edit and delete unwanted photos in Image Viewer.

Adjusting Settings and Taking Photos

As soon as you take a picture, a thumbnail of that photo appears next to the camera button. You can tap that thumbnail to review the picture you have taken and browse other photos.

1. Tap the Image Viewer to review the image.

2. The image opens full screen, the controls appear, and then they fade away. Tap the middle of the screen to access the controls again.

3. Tap the Share Via icon to access many option for sharing your photos through services such as Group Cast, ChatON, Dropbox, Wi-Fi Direct, Picasa, Photo Editor, Google+, Bluetooth, Gmail, and email. The button next to the Share Via icon displays the last option you used to share photos.

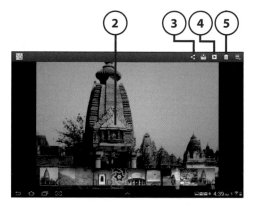

4. Tap Slideshow to begin a slideshow of your photos. After the slideshow begins, you can tap anywhere onscreen to end the slideshow.

5. Tap to delete the currently displayed photo.

6. Tap to access the menu for more options.

7. Tap Face Tag to set whether Camera looks for a face in the current picture.

8. Tap to copy the current image to the clipboard.

9. Tap to rotate the photo to the left.

10. Tap to rotate the photo to the right.

11. Tap to crop the currently displayed photo.

12. Tap to have the option of editing the photo in Photo Editor, Photo Studio, or Video Maker.

13. Tap Set Picture As to set the current picture as a contact photo, Home and lock screens, lock screen, or wallpaper.

14. Tap to share the photo using face detection.

15. Tap to print the photo, such as to a Bluetooth printer.

16. Tap to give the currently displayed image a new name.

17. Tap to connect to other nearby devices.

18. Tap to view details about the photo including the time it was taken, aperture, and exposure settings upon capture.

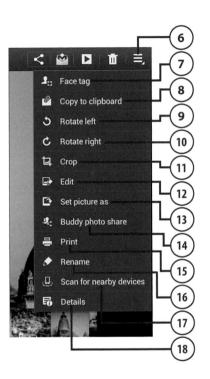

19. With the menu closed, double-tap the image to enlarge it. You can double-tap it again to return it to its normal size. You can also touch the screen with two fingers and then move them apart to enlarge an image.

20. Flick the image from left to right or tap the thumbnail representations of photos at the bottom of the screen to navigate through all the photos you have captured.

21. Tap the Back arrow to return to Camera and take more pictures.

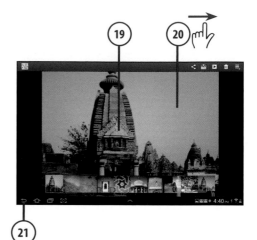

Tips for Capturing Photos

Shutter lag is the amount of time between pressing the shutter release button and the moment the picture is taken. A longer shutter lag is common among most compact cameras and also the Galaxy Tab 2. What this means for you is that is that you have to be particularly mindful of timing your shots when recording moving subjects. Shutter lag can cause you to miss out on a key action if you do not anticipate the shot.

One important thing to know about your Tab is that the shutter does not fire as you place your finger down on the Camera button; the shutter fires when you lift your finger off the button. Use this knowledge to your advantage by pressing your finger on the shutter button and holding while you frame the shot and focus on an object about the same distance as where the subject will pass, to anticipate the shot, and then lift your finger. This means you need to hold your Tab completely still for a little bit longer. Anticipating moving subjects to capture dynamic, moving shots can take some practice.

The Galaxy Tab's slow shutter makes it prone to producing blurry photos if you do not remain perfectly still during capture. Even the smallest movement can have an adverse effect on your photographs; this is especially true in low-light situations. A photo might appear to be fine when you review it on the Tab display, but when you download it and view it on a larger display, you can see the problem.

Working with Gallery

Gallery offers a more robust photo and video management system than Image Viewer, but it has similar options for viewing, sharing, and editing photos.

Managing Photos with Gallery

By default, you can access the Gallery icon by flicking the main Home screen from left to right, or you can access it from the Apps menu.

1. On the main Home screen, scroll from left to right and then tap Gallery.

2. Content is arranged in categories/albums. If you have downloaded videos, such as video podcasts or recorded videos, with your Tab and transferred images from your computer, they are in here, too. Tap the camera icon to access the Camera feature from Gallery.

3. Tap the Albums menu to group your photos and videos in other ways. The name of this particular menu changes depending on which grouping method you have selected.

4. Tap the Albums option to arrange photos based on the folder in which they are stored.

5. Tap Locations to arrange photos based on their GPS location.

6. Tap Time to arrange photos based on the time they were captured.

7. Tap Person to arrange photos based on pictures where a face was detected.

8. Tap Group to arrange photos based on the contact group of the person in the picture.

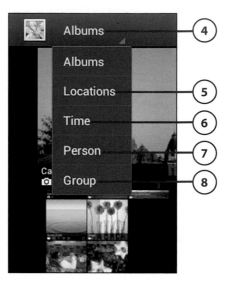

9. Tap the Menu icon to choose Select Album, which enables you to select one or more complete albums to stream to another device, share, or delete. You can also hold your finger to an album for a few seconds to select it.

10. Tap to share photos with nearby devices.

11. Tap View By to view all albums by All Content, Content in Device, and Content in Facebook.

12. Tap an album to view all photos in it.

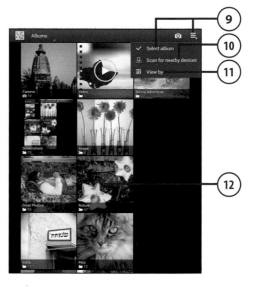

13. After you have captured many photos and videos, the thumbnail representation of images in this category becomes long. Flick the screen right to left and left to right to view all thumbnails in the album.

14. Tap the Camera icon to capture another photo.

15. Tap Slideshow to view a slideshow of pictures. The first frame of any video that you have shot also plays in the slideshow. You can tap the screen again to stop the slideshow.

16. Tap the Menu icon to reveal the options Select Item and Group By. Select Item enables you to select one or more items that you want to stream to another device, share, or delete. The Group By option enables you to change the way albums are grouped. Your choices are to group by Location, Time, or Tags.

17. Touch and hold your finger to a photo to reveal more Gallery options.

18. To delete images within an album, touch each image you want to delete. A green box appears around the image. The number of items you selected appears at the top of the screen. You can touch that number to reveal the option to Select All photos in the album.

19. Tap the trashcan to delete the selected photos.

Select all photos within the album

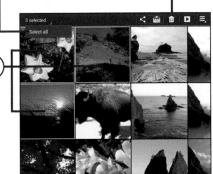

20. Select multiple images within an album and then tap the menu icon to rotate each to the right or left at the same time.

21. Tap a photo in the album to open it full screen.

22. Touch the middle of the screen to reveal the controls.

23. Tap Share to view options for sharing the displayed image with friends and family.

24. Tap the Back arrow at the top of the screen to return to the previous screen.

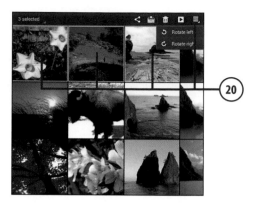

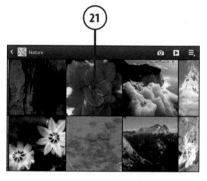

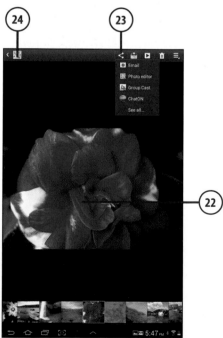

Emailing Photos from Gallery

Emailing your photos to friends and family can be accomplished in just a few taps on your Galaxy Tab.

1. With the album open that has the photo you want to email, touch and hold your finger to that photo to access more Gallery options.

2. Touch more photos that you want to share. A green box appears around each photo, letting you know that it is selected. Email providers have varying file size limitations, so make sure you are aware of your provider's limitations before emailing photographs.

3. Tap the share icon to access the options. You can access these same Share options even if you are viewing a single photo, full screen. Keep in mind that as you add an email account or Facebook account on your Tab, those options also display in this menu.

4. Tap See All to view more options.

5. Tap the Gmail app icon or Email. The mail application opens with the images you selected attached. Notice that the last options you chose in this menu appear to the right of the Share icon. If a Tip window opens after you make a selection, you can just tap OK to close the tip.

6. Tap the X located to the far right of each attachment field to remove the attachment. Keep in mind that you do not have the option to attach a new image at this stage, if you choose to remove an attachment.

7. Type the recipients email into the To field.

8. Tap in the next field and then type a subject for the email.

9. Tap in the body of the email to compose a message.

10. Tap Send to send the email.

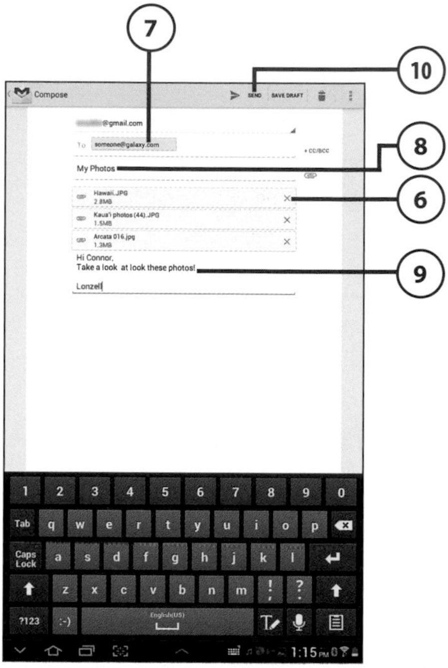

EMAILING FROM CAMERA

You can also email a photo from Camera within Image View. After you tap the Camera button to capture the image, a thumbnail of the image appears in the Image Viewer. Tap the Image Viewer to review the image, and then tap the Share icon to access your email. Email providers have varying file size limitations, so make sure you are aware of your provider's limitations before emailing photographs.

>>>Go Further

Performing Screen Captures

You Galaxy Tab 2 has a very helpful feature that enables you to take screen captures of its interface. The ability to take screenshots can come in handy for educational purposes, especially if you want to post a few Galaxy Tab tips online. Taking a screenshot is as simple as tapping a single button at the bottom of a screen.

Taking Screen Captures

The Screen Capture option is on the System Bar. The System Bar is located at the very bottom of your Galaxy

ess of which

g, or which page

imply tap the

on to capture an

page.

en that you want to

shot of and position the Tab into the orientation in which you want to grab the screen capture: vertical or horizontal.

2. Tap the Screen Capture icon located in the System Bar. You hear the shutter sound effect as it takes the screen capture.

3. The screenshot opens in a photo editor. Tap the checkmark at the top of the screen to save the image. The screenshot is saved to the Screenshots folder in Gallery, and the image is also saved to the clipboard.

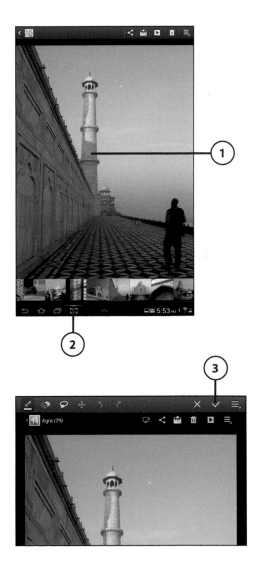

It's Not All Good

DIFFICULTIES TAKING SCREEN CAPTURES

It might not be possible to capture some of your Tab's menus using the Screen Capture function. For example, access the Quick Settings menu by tapping the notification icons at the bottom right of the screen. Now, tap the Screen Capture button. The Quick Settings close and the screenshot is not captured.

Editing Images

Your Galaxy Tab 2 enables you to make some basic photo edits without having to use a third-party photo-editing application. You can improve some photos by performing simple edits such as cropping.

Cropping

You can perform a basic photo edit such as cropping right on the device, which makes it easy for you to further define your photographic subject . You can crop a photo in no time and make huge improvements to photos that were less than perfectly framed.

This section presumes you have already opened Gallery.

1. Tap an album that contains a picture that you want to crop and then tap the picture.

2. Tap the screen to reveal more Gallery options.

3. Tap the menu icon.

4. Tap Crop. A blue overlay appears in the center of the picture.

5. Drag each side of the blue overlay to designate which parts of the image you want to keep.

6. Tap Done to save the newly cropped image.

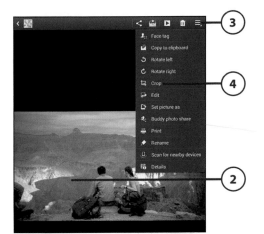

Non-Destructive Edit

When you crop an image, a new copy is made reflecting the edits you have made. The original captured image is untouched.

7. Tap X to cancel the edit.

MORE PHOTO EDITING OPTIONS

>>>Go Further

Photo Editor and Photo Studio offer many more options for enhancing your photographs and they are installed on your Tab when you purchase it. In Photo Editor you find options to rotate, resize, crop, color, and add effects. Spot healing is also an option, which can allow you to retouch blemishes in your photographs. Photo Studio enables you to add effects filters to enhance your photos. Some of these filters have more practical purpose, such as Auto Fix, which attempts to auto enhance your photos without requiring you to make manual adjustments. Other effects are for style such as Film Grain, FishEye, Vintage, and more. You can send your photos from Gallery and Image Viewer to Photo Editor or Photo Studio by opening a photo full screen, tapping the Menu icon, and then selecting Edit. A third option in the list that appears is Video Maker. Choose Video Maker to add a photo to a video project.

Share locations
with friends

Search for
locations
and get
directions

Locate
businesses
and quickly
receive more
information
about them

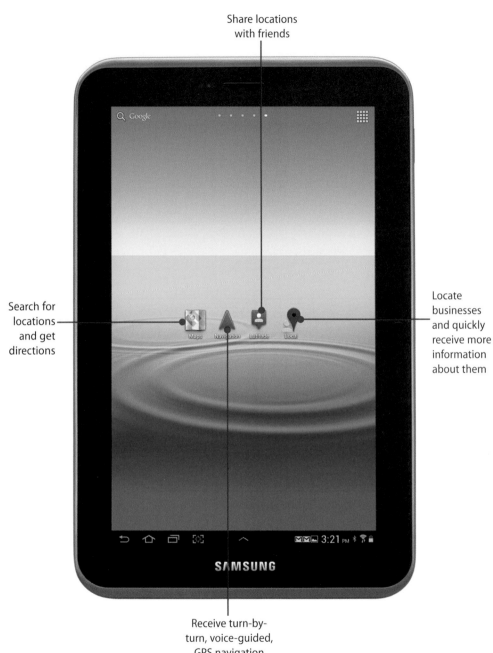

Receive turn-by-
turn, voice-guided,
GPS navigation

In this chapter, you find out how to use the Maps, Navigation, Local, and Latitude apps to find locations, get directions, and connect with friends. Topics include:

→ Enabling GPS

→ Getting around with maps

→ Getting voice-command directions

→ Getting to know Local

→ Enabling wireless networks

→ Using latitude

Using Maps, Navigation, Local, and Latitude

Your Galaxy Tab 2 is equipped with four apps that can help you get where you need to go: Maps, Navigation, Local, and Latitude. Each app helps you accomplish a unique task, yet most of their collective feature base is accessible within each app. Maps can supply detailed destination directions for a specific address. Navigation can provide voice-guided turn-by-turn directions to a location. You can use Local to quickly locate local businesses and access contact information, coupons, and customer reviews. Latitude enables you to share your location with friends and view their locations on a map.

Enabling GPS

Before you can begin to use the many features of your Galaxy Tab 2 that utilize GPS, you must first enable your Tab's GPS capabilities. Activating your Tab's GPS capabilities is a very easy process.

Accessing GPS Through Quick Settings

1. Tap the time in the Status Bar. The Quick Settings appear.

2. Tap GPS into the on position. A green bar appears beneath the setting to indicate that it is on.

Getting Around with Maps

Maps is great for planning a trip across town or the nation. You can change your map view by adding layers that include traffic, terrain, satellite imagery, transit lines, and more. You do not even have to have an address for Maps to help you get where you need to go. Just specify the general area on a map and let the Maps app generate directions on how to get you there.

Finding a Location with Maps

The Maps app on your Galaxy Tab 2 gives you the capability to find locations, get directions, and pinpoint locations. It also gives you access to features in other apps, such as Navigation, Local, and Latitude. The Maps app can help you pinpoint your exact location if you ever find yourself in an unfamiliar place. As soon as you launch Maps, your Tab uses GPS to pinpoint your current location.

Current location

1. Tap Maps on the Home screen.

2. A street map opens displaying your current location

3. Tap Search Maps at the top left of the application bar to find a location. If a Tip window opens, just tap OK to close the window.

4. Type the address of the location you want to find. As you type, a list of possible locations displays.

5. Tap the correct address in the list. Your Tab displays the location on the map. If you cannot find the address you need in the list, Maps might not have complete data for that area or the information might be outdated.

It's Not All Good

INACCURATE OR INCOMPLETE DATA

The Maps application is not always correct. Some of the directions and navigation data that it presents might be inaccurate or incomplete due to change over time. Complete information might not be available for some locations. Always use your best personal judgment and pay attention to road signs, landmarks, traffic conditions, and closures when following directions generated on your Tab.

6. Tap the location overlay.

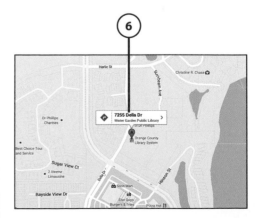

7. Tap the star to the right of the address to save this location for future searches. There are many options you can access from this window including Directions, Street View, and Add as a Contact.

8. Tap the X to close the window.

9. To add additional layers of information to the current map, tap Menu.

10. Tap Layers.

11. Tap the layer of information that you want to add to the map. The information is added to the map, changing the map view.

SWITCHING MAP VIEWS

You can add multiple layers of information to a map by tapping the Layers icon again and choosing another layer. A green check mark is placed next to the layer you have chosen in the list. Tap Clear Map to clear the new layers from the map, or tap More Layers to receive even more map views. You can also view map locations as a satellite image or in Terrain view.

12. Pinch outward to enlarge the map. You can also double-tap your finger in a specific location on the map to enlarge the area. As you move in closer on the map, you start to notice that new information appears in the map, such as the name of banks and restaurants.

13. Use your finger to physically move the map and pinpoint locations.

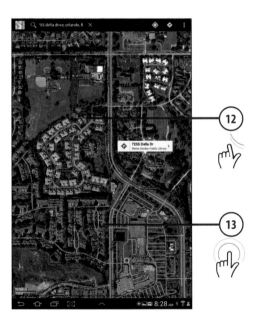

Getting Directions with Maps

Maps can help you get from point A to point B by providing detailed directions. You can get step-by-step driving, public transportation, biking, and walking directions to a specified destination by designating addresses for a starting location and a desired destination.

1. Tap the Maps icon on the Apps screen.

2. A street map opens, displaying your last location searched. Tap the Directions icon at the top-right corner of the screen.

3. By Default, your Tab is able to pin-point your current location, which appears as My Location in the top field. You can also type a different starting address in the top field. As you type, suggested addresses appear in a list below the box; you can tap an address in the list to place that address in the box.

4. By default, the address you searched for appears in the End Point box. You can change the address by tapping in the box and typing a new address. As you type, suggested addresses appear in a list below the box; tap an address in the list to place that address in the box.

5. By default, the car button is select-ed so you can determine how long your trip will take by car. You can also select how long the trip will take by bus, bicycle, or walking.

6. Tap Go to receive directions. A screen of detailed directions appears as a list. The estimated travel time is displayed at the top of the page.

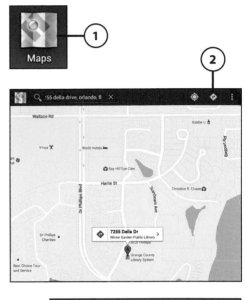

>>>Go Further

USING CONTACT INFORMATION AS LOCATIONS

If you want to use the address information you have for a contact as a Start or End Point, tap the icon that looks like a bookmark located at the end of each field. You can then choose Contacts from the menu.

>>>Go Further

BOOKMARKING LOCATIONS

Each time you generate directions within maps, they are bookmarked under the Layers menu. To use these bookmarked directions, tap Menu, choose Layers, and then tap the location for which you want to generate directions.

7. Scroll up and down the Directions list to move through each step in the directions.

8. Tap Navigate to receive step-by-step voice commands to the destination. This is a great hands-free driving option when coupled with a vehicle mount. (You learn how to use Navigate later in this chapter.)

9. Tap any step in the directions to review it on the map.

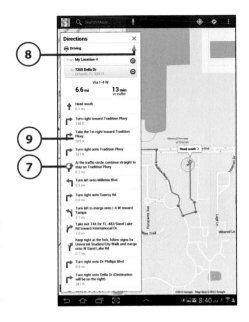

UPDATING/MODIFYING DIRECTIONS

After Maps generates the directions, you can instruct Maps to generate new directions that avoid highways and toll roads. Tap the Menu button on your Tab and then choose Route Options to designate which options you want. Tap OK for updated directions.

>>>Go Further

Specifying Locations with Maps

Maps can also help you find locations for which you do not have an address. For example, you might know that a café that you would like to visit is located downtown, but you do not know how to get downtown from your hotel. Maps enables you to specify a vicinity on a map where you want to go and generates directions from your current location.

1. Tap Maps on the Home screen.

2. Tap the Directions icon.

3. Use My Location as a starting point. If My Location is not currently selected in the first field, tap the Bookmark icon located to the right of the field to select the My Location option from a menu. Maps uses GPS to pinpoint your current location.

4. Tap the Bookmark icon located to the right of the End Point field.

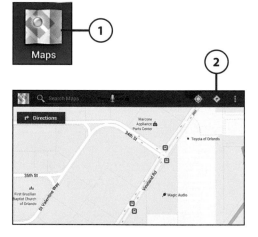

It's Not All Good

CURRENT LOCATION UNAVAILABLE

Occasionally, your Tab might not be able to pinpoint your current location because of lack of area coverage or a temporary disruption in the system. If for some reason Maps gives you the Your Current Location Is Temporarily Unavailable warning, you might have to enter your location by hand.

5. Tap Point on Map so that you can specify a location on the map for which you do not have an address. You are taken to the map.

6. Navigate to the area on the map for where you want to specify a location, and tap an area on the map. An overlay instructs you to Tap to Select This Point.

7. The point you tapped on the map appears in the End Point box. If you want, cut this text and replace it with a new address.

8. Driving directions are generated by default. Select the type of direction you need if you need one of the alternatives.

9. Tap Go to receive the directions.

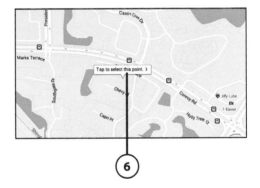

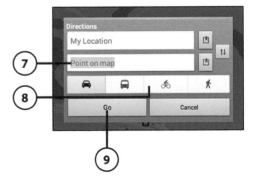

>>>Go Further

ANOTHER WAY TO SPECIFY AN UNKNOWN LOCATION

You can navigate to a location in a map view and then hold your finger down on the area and let Maps generate the address for you. After Maps provides the information for that specified area, tap the information overlay to receive directions, search the nearby area, or share that place via messaging, email, Bluetooth, and more.

Getting Voice-Command Directions

The Navigation app enables you to turn your Galaxy Tab into a turn-by-turn voice-command GPS device. You can take full advantage of your Tab's GPS capabilities by investing in a Galaxy Tab 2 7" Vehicle Power Adapter and Vehicle Mount. The vehicle mount enables you to attach your Tab to the windshield or dashboard. Using the Navigation app for voice-command directions is quite easy.

Receiving Voice Directions

1. If you have purchased a vehicle adapter, use it to power the device.

2. On the Home screen, tap the Apps icon.

3. Tap Navigation.

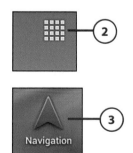

4. Read the important message in the Navigation dialog box. If you want this message to show the next time you open the Navigation app, you can tap in the check box area to tap the Show This Message Next Time check box.

5. Tap Accept. Behind the scenes, Navigation searches for your current location. The Navigation home screen displays.

6. Driving directions are selected by default. Tap the car icon in the application bar to change to walking directions, if needed.

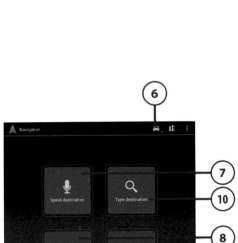

7. Tap Speak Destination to speak the destination into your Galaxy Tab 2.

8. Tap Contacts to pick an address associated with a contact as a destination.

9. Tap Starred Places to choose a previous destination you have starred.

10. Tap Type Destination to type the name of the destination for which you need directions. The Destination field appears at the top of the screen.

11. If a tip window opens, just tap OK to close the window. Tap in the field and type the destination for which you want to receive directions. As you type, possible destinations appear as a list below the field.

12. Tap the correct destination in the list.

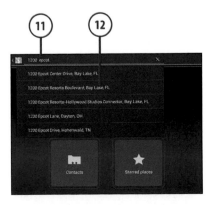

13. Your Galaxy Tab 2 searches for a GPS signal. After a connection is made, a street map appears with a highlighted route and the Navigation app speaks the first set of directions.

14. Attach your Galaxy Tab 2 to the vehicle mount in your car.

15. Drive the route. Much like a dedicated GPS, your Tab senses where you are on the route and proceeds to give you instructions, verbally and graphically.

16. Tap Route and Alternatives to view information about the route and alternative routes.

17. Tap the Directions List to view directions as a step-by-step list.

18. Tap Layers to add information to the map, such as Traffic view, Satellite view, Parking, Gas Stations, ATMs & Banks, and Restaurants.

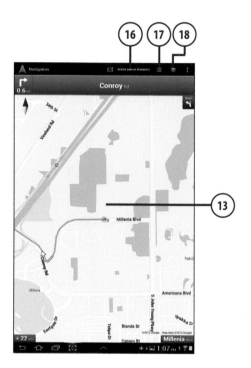

Exploring Route Options

You can access alternative routes from the Route Info screen. You can compare different route options by reviewing their distances in miles as well as overall travel times and highlighted map routes.

>>>Go Further

VIEWING THE MAP

You can find the current step in the directions at the very top of the screen. In the top-left corner, you can view the direction for which you are to travel in the current step, as well as the estimated traveling distance for completing the step. Directions take the form of a left turn arrow, straight arrow, right arrow, or a U turn. In the upper-right corner, you find the direction for your next move. In the lower-left corner of the screen, you find the estimated travel time to your destination.

19. Tap the Menu to access more navigation options.

20. Tap to turn off the navigation voice.

21. Tap to exit navigation

22. Tap Search to find a location.

23. Tap Set Destination to enter a new destination.

24. Tap Settings to enable or disable the power conservation feature of screen dimming between instructions and to read the terms, privacy policy, and notice information.

25. Tap to launch Maps for mobile Help.

Getting to Know Local

Local is a preinstalled app on your Galaxy Tab 2 that enables you to locate places of interest with Google Maps and retrieve information, such as addresses, hours of operation, and phone numbers for those places. You can use Local to pinpoint the exact locations of restaurants, bars, ATMs, gas stations, and more, or you can create a new location, such as pharmacies or hospitals. Local offers a great way to explore nearby areas with which you might not be familiar.

Browsing Local

If you happen to stop in an unfamiliar town, Local is a great app that can help you quickly locate an ATM, a gas station, a hotel, or a place of business. Local uses GPS to pinpoint the nearest specified places and supplies you with directions, telephone numbers, customer reviews, and more.

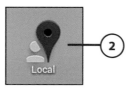

1. Tap Apps on the Home screen.

2. Tap Local.

3. Local pinpoints your current location and displays a list of local establishments in your area. Tap to enter a new address to search what is nearby that location.

4. Tap to sign in to your Google+ account and interact with individuals in your social network.

5. Tap to read recommendations from top reviewers.

6. Tap a category for a place you would like to find in your area and a list of places displays. The places also appear on the map.

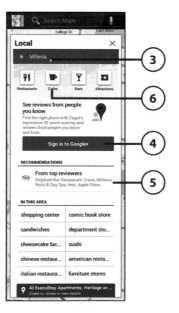

7. Tap Distance to filter the list by ½ mile, 1 mile, 2 miles, 5 miles, or 10 miles.

8. Tap Open Now to filter results to show establishments that are currently open for their business hours.

9. Tap Price to filter the list by the average price of products or services, such as restaurant food.

10. Some places, such as restaurants and coffee houses, have been reviewed by customers. Tap Rating to filter the list by Extraordinary, Excellent, Very Good, and Good reviews.

11. Tap to filter for only coffee shops. Filter options vary depending on which search result you have chosen for your area.

12. Tap the arrows to reveal more filter options.

13. Tap a place in the list to read reviews, write a review, generate directions, view photos, and pinpoint the establishment on a map.

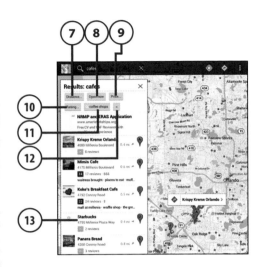

Adding New Places

Can you think of a place that should have been added as a category? Local gives you the capability to add other search categories, such as pharmacies or hospitals. Adding a new place is easy.

1. Tap Apps on the Home screen.

2. Tap Local.

3. Local determines your current location and displays establishments that are nearby. A window of local categories appears. From the Local home screen, tap the Menu.

4. Tap Add a Search to add a category. The Add a Search box displays.

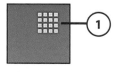

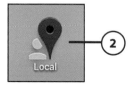

Add a search

Clear Map

Local

Layers

Join Latitude

My Places

Offers

Settings

Help

5. Type a new place in the Add a Search box.

6. Tap Done.

7. The new category appears in the Local window. You can tap the category to bring up a list of places within it.

8. To remove a place category, hold your finger on the category icon until the pop-up menu appears.

9. Tap Remove.

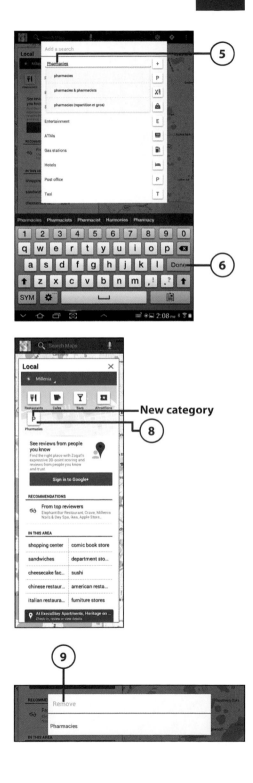

New category

Enabling Wireless Networks

The Google Latitude app enables you to see the location of friends on a map or as a list. You can choose to share your location with others, or hide your location. Before you can use Latitude, you must first configure your Galaxy Tab 2 to use wireless networks and enable Wi-Fi. If the Use Wireless Networks option is not enabled on your Tab, here is how you can turn it on.

Enabling Location Settings

1. Tap Apps on the Home screen.

2. Tap the Apps category.

3. Tap Settings.

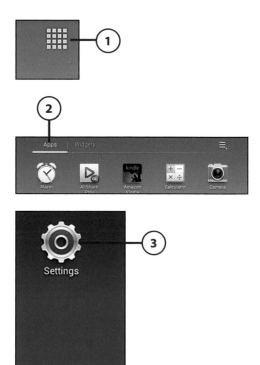

4. Tap Location Services.

5. Tap Use Wireless Networks to enable the setting. A Location consent dialog appears.

6. Read the Location Consent and then tap Agree if you consent.

7. Tap Wi-Fi to the On position.

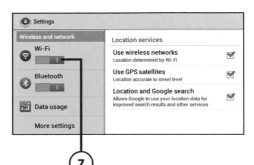

Using Latitude

Adding friends and sharing your locations with others is easy to accomplish after you have enabled your Galaxy Tab 2 to use wireless networks and Wi-Fi. In order to participate, your friends need either a GPS-enabled mobile device or a computer with Latitude installed. Latitude is offered as a feature in Google Maps and can be found on many mobile devices. If a friend decides to use Latitude on a computer, he is also able to share his location automatically if he is connected to a Wi-Fi network and using a supported Internet browser such as Google Chrome.

Sharing Locations

1. Tap Apps on the Home screen.

2. Tap the Apps category.

3. Tap Latitude.

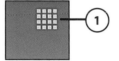

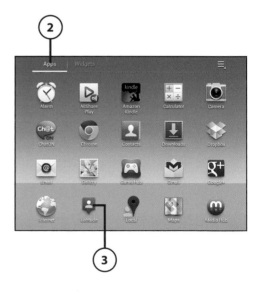

4. The Maps app opens and the Latitude window appears. At first, you are the only friend in the list, but Latitude makes suggestions for friends by searching your contacts.

5. Tap your name to Check In.

6. Tap Check In to tell your friends where you are. If you already have a Google+ account and are logged in to your account, skip to Step 10.

7. You must have a Google+ account in order to check in to places. Tap Continue.

8. Google partially enters your profile information for you. Tap the gender field and select your gender.

9. Tap Continue.

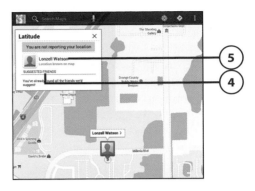

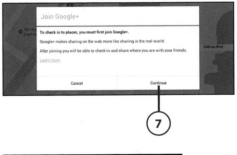

10. A list of nearby locations appears. Tap a location in the list or tap the Search icon in the application bar to type a different location. The search criteria should include the street address, city, and state or province so Latitude can find your location easily. If you find your location in the list, tap the location in the list.

11. Type a comment to your check in.

12. Tap to make your location public.

13. Automatically check in to this location the next time you log into Latitude by tapping the Automatically Check in Here check box.

14. Tap Check in Here.

15. Your location appears as a pin on the map.

16. Tap Latitude.

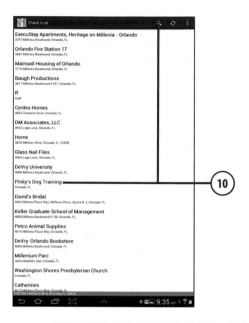

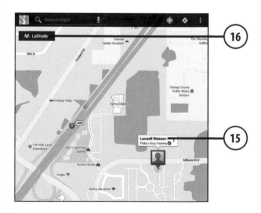

17. Tap to edit your Locations settings including location options, enabling location history, managing your friends and places, and check-in notifications.

18. Tap to Check in to another location and configure location settings.

19. Tap the Menu.

20. Tap to share your location with friends.

21. Tap to check in to locations so that others know your location.

22. Tap to update your list of friends in Latitude.

23. Tap to show or hide friends based on the accuracy of their Latitude information.

24. Tap to configure location reporting settings.

25. Tap to remove search results from the map.

26. Tap Latitude to find your family and friends on a map and share with select people.

27. Tap My Places to display a list of starred places.

28. Tap to edit the Maps settings.

29. Tap to launch Google mobile help.

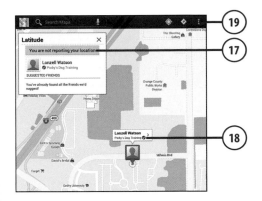

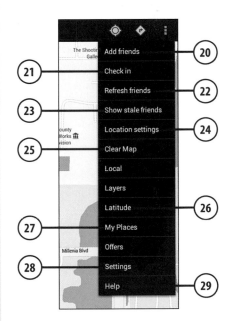

Search Google Play for thousands of useful, educational,
and entertaining apps

In this chapter, you discover how to expand the capabilities of the Galaxy Tab 2 by installing new apps. You also find out how to browse and make purchases on Google Play and organize application icons on your Galaxy Tab. Topics covered in this chapter include:

→ Searching for Android applications
→ Purchasing Android applications
→ Rating applications
→ Getting help with apps
→ Arranging app icons on your Galaxy Tab 2
→ Adding and removing Home pages
→ Adding a dictionary and thesaurus
→ Adding an RSS reader
→ Using the Note Everything app

Enhancing Your Galaxy Tab 2 with Apps

The Galaxy Tab 2 is not just about superior hardware craftsmanship. Your Tab's true strength lies in the incredible software that is developed for it. The Galaxy Tab 2 comes with some truly amazing, preinstalled apps right out of the box, but you can expand its capabilities even further by downloading new apps on Google Play. You can choose from thousands of innovative apps, ranging from games to productivity apps. The number of apps optimized for use on your Tab is growing rapidly.

Getting Apps on Google Play

Google Play makes it easy for you to browse apps and games that you can download to your Galaxy Tab 2. If this is your first time shopping Google Play, you will find the interface quite intuitive. A great way to become acquainted with Google Play is just to start browsing. Many reviews of apps and games are available, so you can make an intelligent choice before downloading. A Google, Bing, or Yahoo! search for "Best Android apps for Galaxy Tab 2" can help you identify the most popular apps. Galaxy Tab 2 users from around the world are writing articles about their experiences with apps that you might find useful. After you download and try out an app, consider giving your feedback so that new Galaxy Tab 2 users can learn from you.

Searching for Android Applications

To access Google Play for the first time, you must use your Google account to sign in to Google Play. After you launch the Play Store app, there are several ways for you to search apps from the home page. The home page search options change position on the page, depending on which orientation you hold your Tab: vertical or horizontal.

1. Tap Play Store on the Home screen.

2. Tap Continue. The Google Play Terms of Service appear.

3. Tap Accept. The Google Play home page displays.

Terms of Service

The Terms of Service appear only the first time you launch Play Store.

4. Tap Apps.

5. Featured applications are listed on the page. Scroll up and down the page to review groups of apps as well as individual apps.

6. Google Play also makes it possible to browse apps by categories, and Top Paid apps. Tap a category to browse the list of results.

7. If you know the name of the app, book, magazine, or movie you want, tap Search Google Play to specify a search term.

8. Type a search term into the field. Possible matches for your search appear in the list below the search field.

9. If the correct product appears in the list, tap the app in the list.

10. The Apps screen shows all results for that app search. For example, the Where's My Perry results page features all versions of that app as well as related apps.

11. Tap an app to go to the description page and read more about the product. You can purchase or freely download the app on the description page.

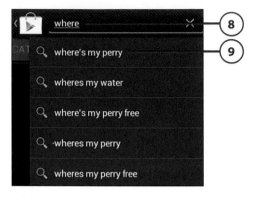

More About Product Descriptions

The description page for an app is chock full of useful information so you can make an educated decision about whether you want to purchase the app. Sample screenshots of the app are featured on this page along with customer reviews and information about the developer.

Other Ways to Search for Apps

Your Galaxy Tab 2 also has the Samsung Apps application preinstalled on the Home screen. You can find many popular free and paid apps for your particular Tab with Samsung Apps. By default, your Galaxy Tab 2 has five Home screens. The default Home screen is number 3. If you flick to Home screen 4 you find another way to find popular apps. Suggest recommends popular apps that are compatible for your device. Tap Home screen 4 to view app entries in categories such as Recommended, Guys, Ladies, and Business.

Finding Great Apps

There are thousands of apps that you can download to your Galaxy Tab 2, so use your storage space wisely by finding the great ones. Finding the best apps might be the biggest challenge of all as you wade through your many options. Here are some tips on how to locate the highest-performing apps.

1. After you launch the Play Store app, tap the Apps category.

2. Take a look at the featured apps on the Play Store home page. Keep in mind that large companies, usually with well-established names, tend to dominate the featured list. Lesser-known developers are also producing outstanding apps, so look deeper.

3. Some apps have trial versions you can test drive before purchasing. Look for Lite or Free versions of applications to test before you buy.

4. Tap an app in the Apps list that you want to learn more about.

5. Scroll down to check out customer reviews for products, but don't trust everything you read. Some reviews might not be in-depth or unbiased, and therefore they are less helpful.

6. Scroll down to the bottom of the page and take a look at the Users Also Viewed list. You see apps that are similar along with their ratings next to them. You might find a higher-rated app that you want to look into.

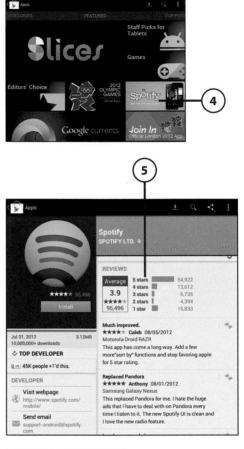

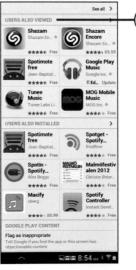

USING OTHER RESOURCES TO FIND APPS

>>>Go Further

You can use other solid resources outside the Play Store for finding great apps.

Perform a Google search—For example, if you are looking for an app suited for taking dictation, type "Galaxy Tab 2 App Dictation."

Search for sites that feature and post reviews for apps—Be aware that some of these sites are sponsored by the developers and might not convey completely objective views.

Find a Galaxy Tab forum—There are many of these popping up every day. In a forum, you can post questions to other Galaxy Tab 2 owners regarding apps. Be aware that experienced Tab users might not moderate all of these forums, and the advice you receive can be questionable.

Purchase Android Applications

Software developers from around the world have developed thousands of apps for you to take advantage of with your Galaxy Tab 2. You can choose from many free apps on Google Play as well as from a variety of more sophisticated apps for a fee. The process for downloading free apps and paid apps is similar, but you need to designate a payment method to make purchases.

1. Tap Play Store on the Home screen.

2. Locate and then tap the app that you want to download. The product description page opens.

More About Product Descriptions

The description page for an app is chock full of useful information so that you can make an educated decision on whether you want to purchase the app. Sample screen-shots of the app are featured on this page along with customer reviews and information about the developer. Be sure to tap at the bottom of the brief descrip-tion on the page so that you review the complete description.

3. Tap the price of the app to see the permissions for this app. If this app is free, tap the Install button.

4. Tap See All to review all permis-sions for the app.

Accepting Permissions

If the application you have selected requires control of your Tab or access to data, Google Play displays the information in this area. The list of permissions changes from app to app. When you accept permissions, you are essentially allowing the applica-tion you are purchasing to access your Galaxy Tab 2, including Internet access.

5. Tap to read the Terms & Conditions.

6. Tap to place a check mark and agree to the Terms and Conditions.

7. Tap to change payment informa-tion, if needed.

8. Tap Accept & Buy to begin install-ing the app.

9. Tap Open to Launch the
    application.

UPDATING APPS

Google Play periodically searches for updates for apps that have been
downloaded to your Galaxy Tab 2. If an update has been found, a notifica-
tion appears in the status bar, located in the bottom-right corner of your
Tab. You can tap the time located in the Status bar to access the Quick
Settings, and then tap the item in the Notifications list to be taken to
Google Play so you can begin the update.

DISABLING UPDATE NOTIFICATIONS

If you prefer to manually check for updates, you can configure Google Play
to stop notifying you about updates. Just launch the Google Play app and
press then tap the Menu icon in the top-right corner of the Application
Bar. Select Settings in the menu, and then deselect the Notify Me About
Updates to Apps or Games That I Download option. You can tap the
Download icon in the top-right corner of the Application Bar to view a list
of installed apps. The list of installed apps also lets you know which apps
have an update that is available. You can also enable the Allow Automatic
Updating setting within this list.

Rating Applications

Rating content you have purchased on Google Play helps others make educated decisions about their purchases. Google Play uses a five-star rating system to rate all content. Much of the content on Google Play features reviews that you can read to see how others like the product. You can easily write reviews of your own to make your feelings known about the content you have purchased.

1. Tap Play Store on the Home screen.

2. Tap the Download icon.

3. Tap Installed to see a list of all of the installed apps on your Tab.

4. Tap the app that you want to rate.

5. Tap to access the description page.

6. Tap Rate & Review.

7. Tap in the Title for Your Review field.

8. Enter a title for your review.

9. Enter your comments.

10. Tap a rating star on a scale from one to five. For example, if you tap the second star from the right the first four stars from left to right are highlighted in blue, which signifies that you give the app a four out of five-star rating.

11. Tap Submit.

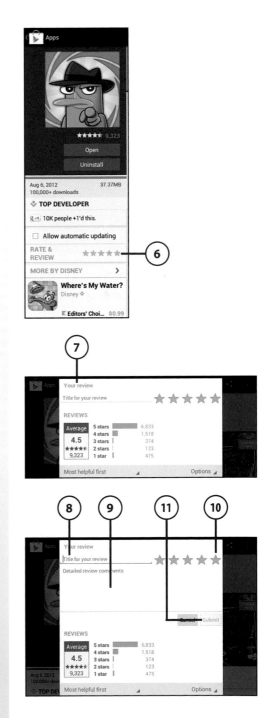

Getting Help with Apps

New applications are being developed for the Galaxy Tab 2 every day. Many new apps are being added on Google Play daily from well-known companies, small companies, and individual developers. Bugs and other problems are likely to arise in such a fast-moving market. There are ways for you to contact developers so that you can ask questions.

1. Tap Play Store on the Home screen.

2. Tap the Download icon.

3. Tap Installed to see a list of all of the installed apps on your Tab.

4. Tap the app for which you need help.

5. Tap to access the description page.

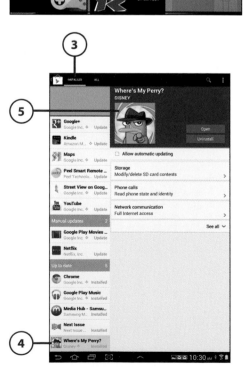

6. Scroll down and tap Send Email in the Developer field to compose an email message asking your question(s).

7. Tap Visit Webpage to visit the developer's site and search for information.

Managing Apps Through Your Home Pages

You begin many of your activities on the Home screen of the Galaxy Tab 2. As you purchase new apps, the number of icons in your Applications menu multiplies, which might prompt you to rearrange them according to the ones you use the most. You can manage your apps through your home pages by creating new home pages, deleting existing home pages, and grouping and arranging apps as you see fit on respective pages.

Arranging Application Icons on Your Galaxy Tab

By default, when you download an application from Google Play, a shortcut is placed in the Applications menu, which is accessible from any Home screen. You can easily move shortcuts from the Applications menu to a Home screen and then rearrange them.

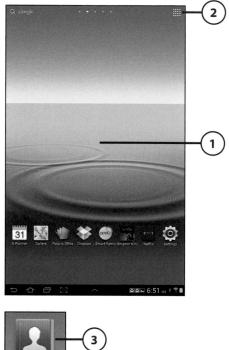

1. Go to one of the five Home screens to place the shortcut. It's easier to place the shortcut on a new screen if you first navigate to screen you want, before you select the shortcut. The default Home screen (Home screen 3) is already filled. You would need to move a current shortcut and replace it with another.

2. Tap Apps on the Home screen.

3. Locate the application shortcut, or widget, that you want to use, and then press and hold your finger on it. An overlay of the Home screen that you chose appears.

4. Move the shortcut to the desired location on the Home screen, and then release your finger. The shortcut is placed on the Home screen.

5. Repeat Steps 2 and 3 to move more App shortcuts from the Applications menu to the Home screen.

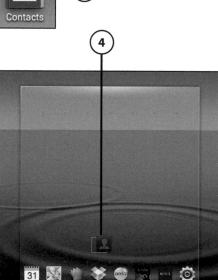

ADD TO HOME SCREEN

A quick way to add widgets, apps, folders, and new pages is to use the Add to Home feature. Press your finger on an empty space on a Home screen and hold until the Home screen menu pops up. Tap Add to Home screen and then choose the options that you want and follow the prompts to complete the task.

6. By default, your Galaxy Tab has five Home screens. Press your finger on a shortcut on a Home screen that you would like to move to another Home screen.

7. Drag the icon with your finger to the edge of the screen to move to another Home screen (in this example, Home screen 2).

8. Remove your finger from the shortcut when you reach the spot where you would like to leave the shortcut.

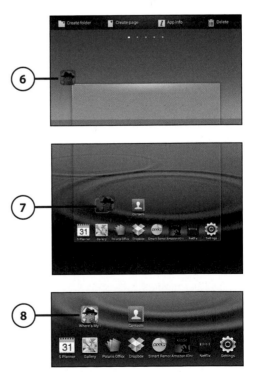

>>>Go Further

CUSTOMIZING HOME SCREENS

Each Galaxy Tab 2 can be customized as unique as its individual owner. You can arrange your icons on any Home screen for shortcuts or widgets that you frequently use. For example, you can arrange all your games on one Home screen panel and all your productivity apps on another. You can even create new panels by tapping the Menu button located on your Galaxy Tab, from any Home screen, and tapping Edit.

9. When you hold your finger on a shortcut and after it pulsates once, the Delete icon (a trashcan) appears in the top-right of the screen. Drag a shortcut to the Delete icon to remove it from a Home screen.

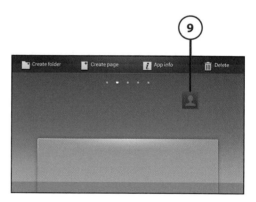

Removing Shortcuts and Widgets

When you remove a shortcut or widget icon, it does not delete or uninstall the app from your Galaxy Tab 2; it simply removes it from that panel. If you want to create a shortcut for that application again, it is still located in the Applications menu, or you can use the Add to Home Screen function.

>>>Go Further

UNINSTALLING APPS FROM YOUR TAB

After you purchase an app from Google Play, you own it forever. You can uninstall a paid app from your Galaxy Tab 2 and then choose to reinstall it later (at no additional charge) in the future. To uninstall an app, tap the Apps icon on a Home screen and then tap Settings. Tap Applications Manager, and choose All to view a list of your applications. Tap the app that you want to uninstall to open the App info and then tap Uninstall. You can also uninstall apps by using the Uninstall option for the application on Google Play.

Working with Widgets

Widgets are a truly valuable aspect of the Android platform. A widget is a small portable piece of code that you can interact with like a minia-ture application. Your Galaxy Tab 2 has quite a few widgets for you to choose from that can make your Tab experience even more convenient. There are many different widgets for different tasks. Tapping a widget can provide you a wide variety of infor-mation such as Stock Market news or the weather. By default, you have a weather widget on your Home screen (page 3). A widget can also act as a world clock or initiate func-tionality from a parent app, such as Maps, when you tap it. You can apply widgets to a Home screen much like an app shortcut, but some widgets must be configured.

1. Go to the screen where you would like to place a widget and then tap the Applications icon.

2. Tap Widgets.

3. Scroll left and right through the five pages of widgets.

4. Locate the widget that you want to use and then press and hold your finger on it. This example uses the Dual Clock widget. An overlay of the Home screen that you chose appears.

5. Move the widget to your desired location on the Home screen and then release your finger. The widget is placed on the Home screen.

6. This Dual Clock (analog) widget lets you configure the information that it displays. Tap the plus sign to set the city.

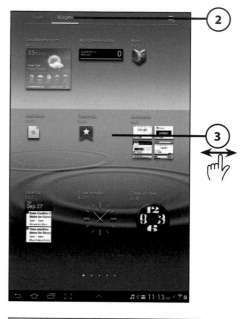

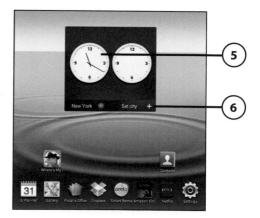

7. Perhaps a friend has traveled to Rome for the summer and you don't want to call her in the middle of the night. Tap Rome.

8. Rome is added to the clock, and now you know the current time for the city where your friend is staying.

9. Tap either city to change to a different city.

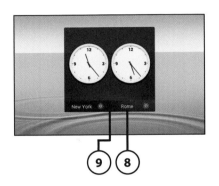

Adding Useful Apps

The true power of the tablet revolution lies not only in the simplification of computing, but also personalization. Apps enable you to optimize your Galaxy Tab for your unique lifestyle. Your Galaxy Tab 2 can be a virtual dictionary or thesaurus. Add an RSS reader and transform your Tab into a news-gathering device so that you are always up to date on current news and events. Many practical apps on the market enhance the capabilities of your Galaxy Tab 2, freeing you from having to purchase and carry a second device such as a digital audio recorder or scanner. There are too many options to list them all here, but let's explore a few practical apps that you might want to consider.

Adding a Dictionary

Adding a simple dictionary app to your Galaxy Tab is a very handy and practical solution for having to lug around an actual paper reference book.

The Merriam Webster Dictionary app is free on Google Play and delivers content that is trusted. The following steps presume you have already downloaded the Merriam Webster Dictionary app from Google Play.

1. Tap the Dictionary app on the Home screen.

Use Any Dictionary App

There are many other free options for dictionary and thesaurus reference apps out there. If you prefer another, don't hesitate to use it. This is just a recommendation for the usefulness of such a reference to exist on your Galaxy Tab 2. The Dictionary.com app is also a great application and gets the job done.

2. Tap in the Search box and enter a word to look up. Search suggestions appear beneath the field.

3. Tap the correct search. The definition(s) for the entry appear.

4. You can tap the speaker icon to hear the pronunciation of the word.

5. Tap to speak a new word to search.

6. Tap to expand the definition to full screen.

7. Tap the star to add this word to your Favorites.

8. Tap to view a list of recently searched words.

9. Tap to view all words you have marked as Favorite.

10. You can learn a new word every day. Tap to view the word of the day.

11. Tap to provide Feedback to the developers of this app, rate this app, and share this app. You also find information about Merriam-Webster and list of similar recommended apps such as the Britannica Encyclopedia.

Adding an RSS Reader

If part of your daily routine includes reading news websites and blogs, adding an RSS reader can help you manage your news sources from one app in the form of feeds instead of visiting multiple websites. Pulse is a free RSS feed reader that you can download from Google Play; it enables you to acquire and manage multiple news feeds as an interactive mosaic. The following steps presume you have already downloaded the Pulse app from Google Play.

1. Tap Pulse. Pulse navigation tips appear as scribble.

2. Tap the screen to dismiss the tips.

3. Pulse is loaded with predefined news feeds to get you started. Each row represents an individual news feed. Flick to the left in a news feed to view the rest of the news items for the feed.

4. Tap the Menu to enter the settings and Refresh All news feeds.

5. Hold your finger to the name of a feed to type a new name.

6. Tap to choose a new feed to add to the page.

7. Tap a news story to open it.

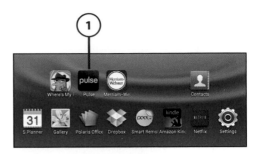

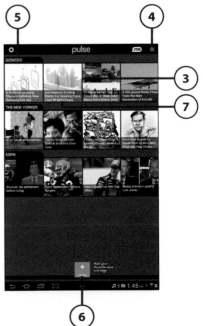

REFRESHING AUTOMATICALLY

You can choose an automatic refresh option by tapping the Menu icon and then selecting Settings to access the Data Sync menu.

---

8. The news story opens in the window.

Landscape or Portrait Orientation

The Pulse interface options change, depending on whether you hold your Tab in landscape orientation or portrait orientation as shown in these steps. Try holding your Tab in various orientations to see which you prefer.

---

9. Tap to select a new font size for the article text.

10. Tap to leave the article marked as unread, to open the article in a browser, or choose the Default Open Source to Website option, which opens the article on the main website where the article is found.

11. Tap the name of the feed to view the list of other articles for this feed at the bottom of the page.

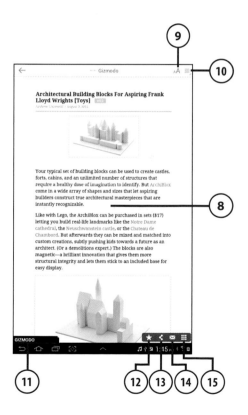

You could then flick through the remaining articles. If you're holding the Tab in landscape orientation, the other articles for this feed would appear to the left of the screen, and the current article to the right.

12. Tap to mark the article as a favorite.

13. Tap to share the article on Facebook, Twitter, and/or Google+.

14. Tap to email the article to a friend.

15. Tap to return to the Pulse home screen of various feeds.

16. Tap Settings.

17. Press your finger to the name of a news feed and drag it to reorder feeds.

18. Tap to add a new page.

19. Search new categories and then choose a new category.

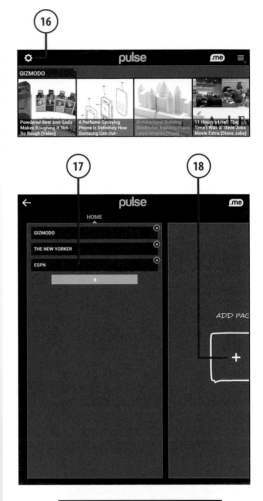

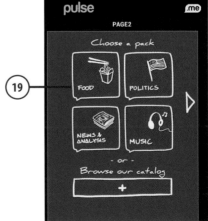

20. The new category appears on the second page.

21. Tap to add more feeds to the new category.

22. Tap an X to delete a feed.

23. Tap the back arrow to view the new page.

Multiple Pages of News Feeds

You can add five pages of news feeds within Pulse. If you choose to populate a new page with feeds you can access the new pages by tapping the various page numbers at the top of each page.

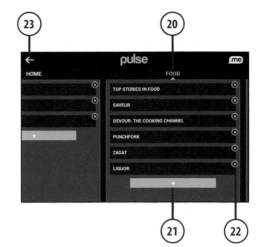

Using Note Everything

A digital voice recorder can be a priceless tool if you ever need to record some notes for yourself. Or have you ever wished you had the capability to scan barcodes on a product so that you could store the information?

Note Everything is a free app that can do all of this and more, including taking handwritten notes and tucking information away neatly in folders. This section presumes you have already downloaded the Note Everything app from Google Play.

1. Tap the Note Everything icon on the Home screen.

Receiving Help

When you first use certain functions, a help screen appears and provides you with tips.

2. Tap Close in the What's New screen.

3. Tap the Menu button in the status bar.

4. Tap New Note.

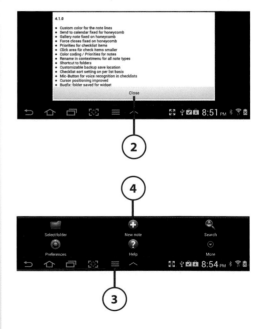

5. Tap Textnote to leave a note using the keyboard. This is similar to how the preinstalled Memo widget works on your Tab, but you might find it more beneficial to have all your notes in one location.

6. Tap Paintnote to leave a note using your finger as a pen. You can tap the Menu button on your Galaxy Tab and change the color of ink, erase marks, change stroke width, clear colors, work full screen, and more. This is a great option for jotting down a quick visual note.

7. Tap Voicenote to record voice memos. Each recording is stored as an individual file that you can play back on your Galaxy Tab.

8. Tap Note from Barcode to use your Galaxy Tab 2 camera to read barcodes and note the barcode for later reference. This option requires you to install another free app named Barcode Scanner for it to work. The installation process is streamlined within the Note Everything app and takes only a few moments.

9. Tap Note from Google Docs to import and export text notes from Google Docs. This option requires you to install another free app named Note Everything (NE) GDocs. These two apps can work seamlessly together or independently.

It's Not All Good

NOT ALWAYS ACCURATE

Be advised that not all barcode scanners on your Galaxy Tab 2 are 100% accurate. That goes for any product, not just the one featured here. Sometimes these scanners might not recognize the product, or the price they provide for the product might be way off the mark. Use all these apps with caution. If you don't like this app, you can choose from many other free options.

Recording Voice Notes

After each recording, you can choose whether to use or discard the recording. If you choose to keep it, you are taken to a page with a notepad where you can play back the voice memo and take text notes at the same time.

10. After you create a note, it is placed in the main (root) menu. Tap and hold your finger on any note that you would like to move to a different folder, and a pop-up menu appears.

11. Tap Move to Folder.

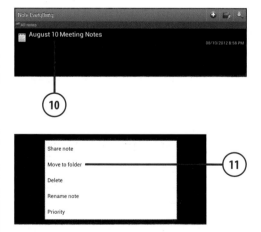

12. Tap Close after you read the help screen. Help screens appear when you access a function for the first time.

13. Tap the Menu button in the status bar.

14. Tap Create Folder.

15. Tap in the Folder Name box to access the keyboard and then enter a name for the folder.

16. Tap OK to move the note to the new folder.

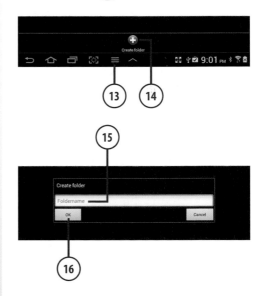

Extend your Galaxy Tab 2
with accessories

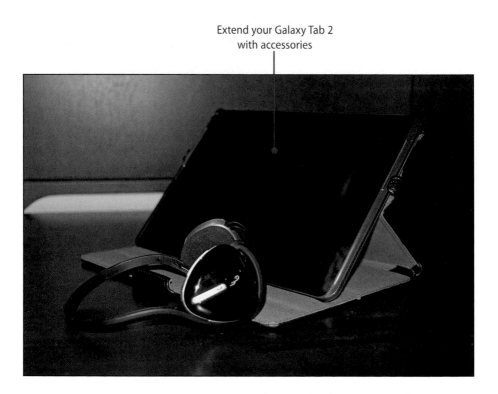

This chapter covers how to get the most from your Galaxy Tab by exploring hardware accessories such as the optional Multimedia Desk Dock, the Keyboard Dock, and memory card options. Accessories covered in this chapter include:

→ Galaxy Tab USB and SD connection kit
→ Bluetooth keyboards
→ Pairing Bluetooth devices
→ MicroSD cards

Adding New Hardware

Your Galaxy Tab 2 is fully capable of providing an amazing multimedia experience right out of the box, but whether you are viewing movies, capturing photos and video, or composing a long email, you want your Galaxy Tab to be versatile. Accessories such as Bluetooth headsets, desk docks, Bluetooth keyboards, and extra memory cards can offer some much needed practical support for your Tab use.

You can find accessories for the 7" and 10.1" Galaxy Tabs in electronics stores such as Best Buy, or you can try your local electronics store. Online stores, such as Samsung.com and Amazon.com, are also great places to find hardware accessories for both Galaxy Tabs. Always make sure that you pick the right accessory for your Galaxy Tab model. As of this writing none of the previous Galaxy Tab accessories work with the Galaxy Tab 2.

Limited Accessories to Date

This section covers accessories that were available as the book was written for both the Galaxy Tab 2 7" and 10.1" devices. We are sure that shortly after this book finds it way onto shelves that there will be new accessories that are not mentioned in this chapter. For example, Samsung does not offer a multimedia desk dock or keyboard dock for the Galaxy Tab 2. I encourage you to keep up to date on what is available for your device by periodically checking the Samsung website, Amazon.com, and tech forums.

Galaxy Tab USB and SD Connection Kit

These two devices are small enough to put in your pocket and they enable your Galaxy Tab 2 7" or 10.1" to connect with compatible USB accessory devices including mice, keyboards, and thumb drives. The SD adapter enables you to transfer files from a micro SD card directly to your Tab's internal storage. You can use these adapters to easily share your favorite multimedia files. Simply insert a USB memory stick or micro SC card into the respective adapter and then insert the adapter into your Tab to transfer the files.

Bluetooth Keyboards

Your Galaxy Tab comes with Bluetooth 3.0 technology, which enables you to use devices such as wireless headphones and wireless keyboards. There are limited third-party companies that produce accessories such as the Bluetooth keyboard for both the 7" and 10.1" Galaxy Tab 2 devices. (One such company is eWonder.) A Bluetooth keyboard provides the convenience of typing with a physical keyboard, which makes it easier to write a lengthy message. This accessory provides a typing experience similar to using a computer keyboard, so inputting information is easier than using the onscreen keyboard. Users who perform extensive writing tasks might find the more ergonomically pleasing Bluetooth keyboard a better alternative to the onscreen keyboard. This accessory is usually in a 2-in-1 package meaning that it serves both as a QWERTY keyboard and also a folding leather protective case. A Bluetooth keyboard case not only protects your Galaxy Tab, but it is also very travel-friendly. You can find eWonder accessories by performing a product search on Amazon.com.

Pairing Bluetooth Devices

Along with the many other comfort features and conveniences found with the Galaxy Tab 2, your Tab gives you the capability to connect some external hardware devices wirelessly. The Galaxy Tab is equipped with Bluetooth 3.0 technology, enabling you to connect cable-free with Bluetooth-capable keyboards and headphones. By default, Bluetooth is disabled on your Tab. If you have already played with this setting, you can tell if Bluetooth is turned on by verifying that the Bluetooth symbol is visible in the status bar at the top of the screen.

Pair a Bluetooth Device

You can easily connect your Tab to a Bluetooth device in two phases: discovering and pairing.

1. Turn on the wireless device that you want to pair with your Galaxy Tab and make it discoverable.

Discoverability

Bluetooth devices broadcast their availability only after you instruct them to do so. If necessary, refer to your device's manual to learn how to make it discoverable.

2. Tap the Apps icon in the upper-right corner of the Home screen.

3. Tap the Apps category.

4. At the bottom of the page, tap Settings in the menu.

5. Tap Bluetooth to view the Bluetooth options to the right of the screen.

6. Tap Off to place the Bluetooth setting in the On position. The switch turns green and any detectable Bluetooth devices are listed to the right.

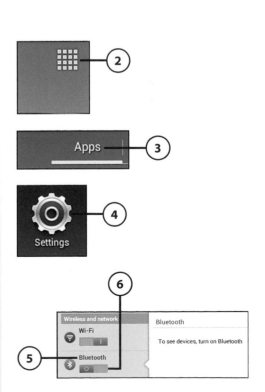

7. Tap your Bluetooth device in the list. Your Tab attempts to pair with the device.

8. The device then appears under a newly created Paired Devices list.

Paired Bluetooth Device Settings

After you have successfully paired your device to your Tab a Settings icon appears next to the name of the Bluetooth device within the Paired Devices list. Tap that Settings icon to rename, unpair, or further configure your device.

When Paired

When a device is paired with your Galaxy Tab, you never have to configure the devices again.

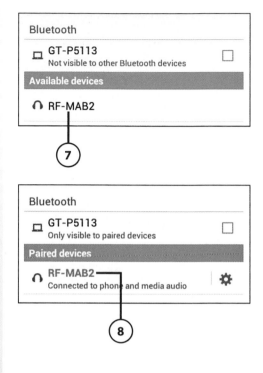

MicroSD Cards

Your Tab supports MicroSD and MicroSDHC memory cards that come in the following sizes: 4GB, 8GB, 16GB, and 32GB. Increasing the storage capacity of your Galaxy Tab 2 is a convenient way to store more music, photos, videos, and other files.

Formatting MicroSD Cards (Galaxy Tab 7")

If you buy a new card, you need to format it for your Galaxy Tab. Whether you are upgrading a MicroSD card or adding a new card, follow these steps to format your new memory card:

1. From a Galaxy Tab Home screen, tap the Apps icon.

2. Tap Apps.

3. At the bottom of the page, tap Settings.

4. Tap Storage.

5. Insert the MicroSD card into your Tab. All of the MicroSD Card information appears under the SD card category to the right.

6. Tap the Format SD card option located at the bottom of the SD card category.

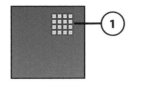

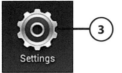

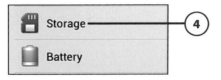

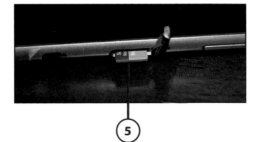

7. Read the warning and then tap Format SD Card.

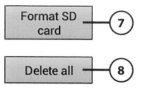

8. Read the warning and then tap Delete All. The SD card is formatted and becomes instantly available for use.

Unmount Before Removing

It is very important that you first unmount the MicroSD card before removing it from the slot. Failing to do so can result in damage to the MicroSD card. Simply tap Unmount SD card in the SD Card category.

Press the card to eject

Extend your Galaxy Tab 2
with docks, cases,
connectors, and keyboards

This chapter offers options on how to accessorize your Galaxy Tab 2 with protective cases, screen protectors, chargers, and adapters. It also covers ways to maximize the longevity of your Galaxy Tab. Accessories covered in this chapter include:

→ Protective cases

→ Screen protectors

→ Chargers and adapters

Finding Galaxy Tab 2 Accessories

There are many accessories available for both the 7" and 10.1" models of the Galaxy Tab 2, ranging from those that increase its usability to those that protect your iPad or enhance its style. You can start on the Samsung website to explore which accessories are right for you, but don't stop there. Many other companies create high-quality accessories for the Galaxy Tab. Amazon.com is a great place to browse the many offerings for the Galaxy Tab and read product reviews from other buyers. Let's take a look at a variety of accessories to see how they can benefit you.

Protective Cases

Perhaps the most fundamental duty you have as a Galaxy Tab 2 owner is to protect your Tab from becoming damaged. There are many cases on the market to choose from, and all provide some degree of protection for your Tab. It is important to note that as of this writing, Samsung does not offer cases for either of the Galaxy Tab 2 devices on their website. Fortunately, there are many third-party vendors you can browse on Amazon.com and other electronic stores that offer a wide assortment of options for your 7" or 10.1" Tab.

Skins are stylish and provide a thin layer of protection around your Galaxy Tab, which can be effective for protecting your Tab against dust, nicks, and scratches. A skin by itself is less effective for absorbing shock, such as from a drop, than a padded case that remains on your Tab at all times.

Some padded cases, such as the Poetic Slimbook Leather Case for the 7" Tab and the Moko Slim-Fit Cover Case for the 10.1" Tab, also act as stands.

1. Fold the front cover of the Case underneath the Tab.

2. Set the Tab down on a flat surface so the screen is in a landscape orientation.

3. Angle the Galaxy Tab display so that it is easy to view. This is a great orientation in which to watch videos or movies.

4. Set the Galaxy Tab up in portrait orientation by positioning the folded cover behind it.

>>>Go Further

ALTERNATIVES TO CASES

Protective cases aren't the only way to keep your Galaxy Tab safe from the elements and damage. Protective pouches, sleeves, or slipcases are other alternatives. If you prefer the tactile experience of the Galaxy Tab body in your hands while you use it, you can use a pouch when you're carrying your Tab and then slip the device from the pouch when you're ready to use it. A leather or cloth pouch can also act as an extra layer of protection for that stylish skin you have been eyeing for your Tab.

Screen Protectors

Most cases, skins, and pouches do not include a protective screen cover to keep your high-resolution screen from getting scratched, so you might have to purchase one separately. You can choose from a variety of protective screens; the most popular are clear (invisible), mirrored, and antiglare.

A clear protective screen performs the basic duty of preventing your Galaxy Tab's glass screen from being scratched or collecting dust. A protective film offers three layers of protection after you apply one using its self-adhering surface, and it's barely noticeable. Some screen protectors, such as the ArmorSuit Military Shield, even protect against moisture and self-heal (minor scratches to the shield's surface repair themselves over time). To remove the protector, just peel off the film.

A mirrored screen does exactly what it says. When your Galaxy Tab screen is off, the screen reflects as a mirror. When the Galaxy Tab screen is on, the mirror goes away. This option not only protects your screen but also adds a stylish aesthetic to your tab. One thing to keep in mind when choosing this option is the glare factor when using your Tab in the sun. A substantial glare can impede screen visibility.

Antiglare screen protectors make it easier for you to view your Galaxy Tab display indoors or outdoors in direct sunlight. While protecting your screen, they also help to reduce annoying surface glare caused by bright indoor lighting.

Chargers and Adapters

The Galaxy Tab 2 was designed for a person who is on the go. Put your Tab 7" in your back pocket or tuck your 10.1" Tab under your arm and go. Many accessories are available to the power user, including additional power chargers and adapters. For example, you might want to charge your Galaxy Tab at the office as well as at home. Instead of remembering to transport a single cable, wall jack, or Dock, why not invest in two? You can also have the convenience of charging your Galaxy Tab while in a car.

- **Galaxy Tab USB Charging/Data Cable**—You can use this data cable to connect your Tab to a PC, Mac, or Samsung charger. This offers a two-in-one solution for charging power and transferring data simultaneously via USB data sync cable. You can also use it to connect your Tab to your computer.

- **Galaxy Tab 30-pin Vehicle Power Adapter with Detachable Cable**— The Samsung Car Adapter, with data cable, enables you to charge your Galaxy Tab while in your car. You can plug it into your car's 12-volt cigarette lighter socket. If you have to transfer data from your Galaxy Tab to your laptop, or vice versa, this car charger provides a detachable USB cable that enables you to connect to your laptop and make the transfer. You can also simultaneously charge your Galaxy Tab through the same connection to your laptop.

- **Galaxy Tab 30-Pin Travel Adapter with Detachable Cable**—Charge your Tab while on the go or at home with this adapter that plugs into any standard wall outlet. This adapter includes a USB port for universal charging and a 2A charger.

>>>Go Further

OTHER CHARGERS AND ADAPTERS

When it comes to accessories, perhaps the biggest decision to make is choosing from the variety of available manufacturers' products. There are many options for the power user, such as worldwide travel plug adapters, mini surge protectors, and dual cigarette lighter sockets. Always make sure that the accessories you use are compatible with your Galaxy Tab 2. Not all manufacturers' accessories are of equal quality.

Troubleshoot Galaxy
Tab software, hardware,
and accessories

This chapter covers ways that you can properly maintain your Galaxy Tab 2 and troubleshoot basic software or hardware problems. Topics covered in this chapter include:

→ Maintaining your Galaxy Tab 2

→ Updating the Galaxy Tab software

→ Backing up and restoring your Galaxy Tab 2

→ Extending battery life

→ Solving Galaxy Tab issues

→ Troubleshooting connected devices

→ Getting help

Troubleshooting Your Galaxy Tab 2

Although problems concerning the Galaxy Tab 2 software, hardware, and accessories are rare, on occasion, you might experience incidents where your Tab does not perform properly. There are a few fixes you can try if you experience the occasional glitch that can occur with any hardware device.

Although your Galaxy Tab 2 is a sophisticated piece of hardware, it is less complex than an actual computer, making any issue that might arise more manageable.

Maintaining Your Galaxy Tab 2

Regular maintenance of your Galaxy Tab 2 not only helps extend the life of your Tab, it also helps ensure peak performance. Making sure your Galaxy Tab 2 software is up to date and understanding basic troubleshooting concepts is important. Properly cleaning and protecting your Tab's body can be equally important. The Galaxy Tab was designed to be sturdy, but, like any other electronic device, it can collect dust, and a simple drop on the sidewalk can prove disastrous. The first step in maintaining your Galaxy Tab is prevention. You can start by purchasing a protective case.

A sturdy case designed for the Galaxy Tab 2 is important for the overall protection of your device. A number of companies have created a variety of cases for the Tab, so search the Internet or go to Amazon.com to see what's out there. The more padded the case, the better it can absorb a shock if you happen to drop your Tab. A case can also help protect your Tab from dust and keep it dry if you happen to get caught in the rain. Make sure that you keep the inside of your case clean. Dust and sand can find its way into even the most well constructed cases. Instead of using your sleeve to wipe off your Galaxy Tab's display, invest in a microfiber cloth; you can find them in any office supply or computer store.

Your first instinct might be to wet a cloth to clean your Galaxy Tab touchscreen. Don't use liquids to clean the touchscreen, especially if they are alcohol and ammonia. These harsh chemicals can cause irreparable damage to the touchscreen, rendering it difficult to see. Consider purchasing a screen protector at your local Best Buy or favorite online retailer to keep the touchscreen dust and scratch free. Some screen protectors also come with a microfiber cleaning cloth.

Update Galaxy Tab 2 Software

Every so often, Google releases software updates for your Galaxy Tab's Android operating system. To get the most from your Galaxy Tab 2, it is good practice to upgrade soon after an upgrade has been released. When an update is available, you receive a notification that indicates that a system upgrade is available. At that point, you have the option to initiate the software update. You can also check for system updates manually by tapping Settings in the Apps menu, tapping About Device, and then choosing Software Update. You are given an option to Check for Updates. If your system is up to date, your Tab alerts you to this fact. If an update is available, follow the provided directions to upgrade your software.

The Android operating system is not the only software you need to update on your Galaxy Tab. Your Tab also uses software, called *firmware*, to run its internal functions. When an update is available, use your own discretion as to whether you want to update right away, just in case there are any issues with the update.

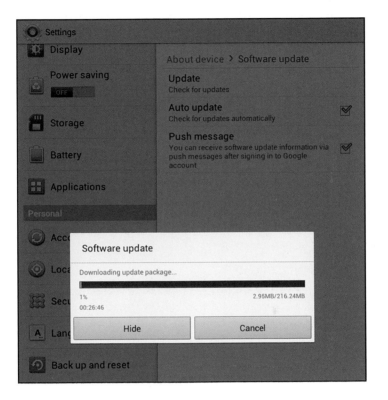

Backing Up and Restoring Your Galaxy Tab 2

Backing up the contents of your Galaxy Tab 2 is a good practice for securing your important information and multimedia content. You can ensure that your contacts, photos, videos, and apps are copied to your PC or Mac in case something happens to your Tab.

Ensuring Automatic Google Account Backup

Your Google account information, such as your Gmail inbox, Contacts list, and Calendar app appointments, automatically sync with Google servers, so this information is already backed up for you. To ensure that your Google account information is being automatically backed up, follow these directions.

1. Tap the Apps icon from any Home screen.

2. Tap Apps.

3. At the bottom of the page, tap Settings.

4. Scroll down and tap Accounts and Sync. Your Google account(s) appear under Manage Accounts.

5. Ensure that Auto-Sync is in the On position.

6. Tap a Google account under Manage Accounts.

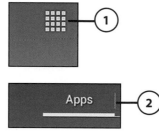

7. Ensure that the Sync Calendar, Sync Contacts, Sync Gmail, Sync Google Photos, Sync Google Play Books, Sync Instant Upload, and Sync Internet fields all have a green check mark to the right. If they don't, tap the box to place a green check mark within the box.

Multiple Google Accounts

If you have multiple Google accounts, repeat Steps 1 through 6 for each account.

8. Tap Back Up and Reset.

9. Ensure that a green check mark appears next to Back Up My Data and Automatic Restore. If not, tap the box in each field to place a green check mark within the box. The information associated with your Google address is now automatically backed up.

The Automatic Restore Option

When checked, the Automatic Restore option ensures that any data or settings placed on third-party apps are restored when you restore those apps to your Galaxy Tab.

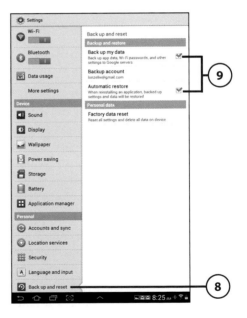

Syncing and Using Manual Backup

There are multiple ways for you to back up content that is outside of your Google account information on your Galaxy Tab 2, such as your apps and multimedia content, onto your computer. Connect your Galaxy Tab 2 to your PC as a mass storage device and manually drag and drop files. You can use the Samsung Kies software to transfer data, synchronize files, and update firmware while connected to a PC or Mac.

When connected to your PC as a mass storage device, you can view all of the data on your Tab's internal storage and optional MicroSD card. The content is categorized into specific folders that you can copy from your card and internal storage such as DCIM, Download, Music, Pictures, Movies, Podcasts, and more. You can also copy all folders with the names of apps installed on your Galaxy Tab 2.

You can also use the Samsung Kies software for PCs and Macs to sync your content. See Chapter 8, "Playing Music and Video," to learn how to exchange content between your Galaxy Tab 2 and your computer by connecting as a mass storage device and by using Samsung Kies.

Extending Battery Life

Your Galaxy Tab 2 is capable of up to 8.5 hours of battery life, but battery life can vary depending on how you use the Galaxy Tab. Strenuous tasks, such as playing HD video, dramatically lower your battery life more than surfing the Web does. You can monitor your battery power at the top of the screen in the Status area. The green battery status icon located in the lower right of the status bar lets you keep an eye on how much battery power you have left. When the battery gets low, a warning appears, informing you of the percentage of battery power you have left and instructing you to connect the charger. When the battery is too low, your Tab automatically shuts down. There are a few things you can do to extend the life of your Tab's battery.

Battery icon

Monitoring Power Usage

On the Galaxy Tab 2 you can use the Battery Usage screen to see which of the apps you use consumes the most power, and then you can reduce the use of those apps. Your battery power savings are small, but if you're running low on power with no way to recharge, every little bit counts. Follow these directions to access the Battery Usage screen.

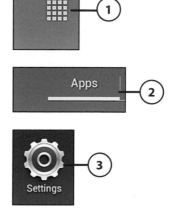

1. Tap the Apps icon on your Galaxy Tab from any Home screen.

2. Tap Apps.

3. At the bottom of the screen, tap Settings.

4. Tap Battery. The screen displays the items that are consuming the most battery power.

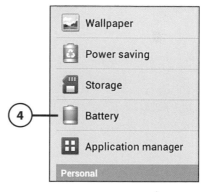

Battery use

Dim Screen Brightness

The high-quality touchscreen of the Galaxy Tab 2 can consume plenty of battery power. The higher the brightness level set on your Galaxy Tab 2 the more power the touchscreen uses. If you are viewing the screen in very bright conditions, you probably do not need a very high brightness setting. Consider dimming the screen to extend the battery life.

Adjust Screen Brightness

It is very easy to adjust the screen brightness for your Galaxy Tab 2. You can use the Settings menu to deselect Auto Brightness and then manually adjust screen brightness to your liking. Follow these directions to dim the screen.

1. Tap the Apps icon.

2. Tap the Apps category.

3. At the bottom of the screen, tap Settings.

4. Tap Display.

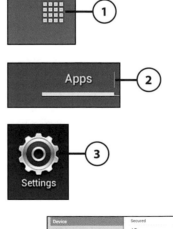

5. Tap Brightness.

6. Tap the Automatic Brightness check box to deselect the Automatic Brightness setting.

7. Slide the slider to the left to lower the brightness level.

8. Tap OK.

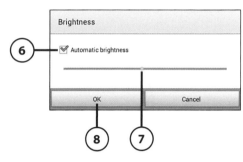

Automatic Brightness

When the Automatic Brightness setting is selected, your Tab uses sensors to determine your current light conditions and then adjusts the screen brightness automatically. In bright conditions, the screen is dimmed, and vice versa.

Quick Settings for Brightness

The Galaxy Tab 2 offers a quicker way for you to access the brightness controls by providing quick settings in the notification panel. Simply tap in the far-right corner of the status bar located at the bottom right of your Tab's screen, deselect the Auto setting, and then use the slider to adjust screen brightness.

Utilize Sleep Mode

Your Galaxy Tab 2 goes to sleep after a specified period of inactivity, but you don't have to wait for it to fall asleep, you can put it to sleep manually. When your Tab is awake, it is consuming battery power. Press the sleep button on the side of your Tab when you have finished using the device to conserve battery power.

Conserve Power by Turning Off Wi-Fi

When the Wi-Fi antenna is activated on your Galaxy Tab, your device is incessantly looking for available Wi-Fi networks to join, which uses battery power. To see if Wi-Fi is turned on, check the status bar in the top-left corner of your Galaxy Tab for the Wi-Fi symbol. If you do not need a Wi-Fi connection, turn it off to conserve battery power. If you are not wandering and are using Wi-Fi in a single location, look for a power outlet and plug in ysour Tab.

Turn Off Wi-Fi

Turn off Wi-Fi in the Settings options under Wireless and Network. Follow these directions to turn off Wi-Fi and help conserve some battery power.

1. Tap Apps from any Home screen.
2. Tap the Apps category.
3. Tap Settings.
4. Tap Wi-Fi to turn off the setting.

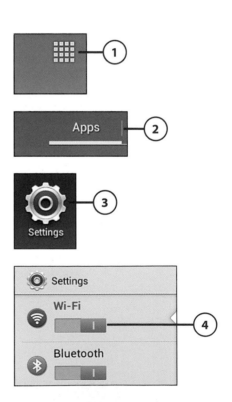

Quick Settings for Wi-Fi

The Galaxy Tab 2 offers an even quicker way for you to access the Wi-Fi setting by providing quick settings in the notification panel. Simply tap in the far-right corner of the status bar located at the bottom right of your Tab's screen and tap the green Wi-Fi setting to turn it off.

Conserve Power by Turning Off Bluetooth

When Bluetooth is activated on your Galaxy Tab, your device is constantly checking for other Bluetooth devices, which drains battery power. To see if Bluetooth is turned on, check the status bar in the top-left corner of your Galaxy Tab for the Bluetooth symbol. If you are not using a Bluetooth device, turn this function off. There are also security reasons why you should turn off Bluetooth when you are not using it, so get in the habit of turning Bluetooth off as soon as you finish using a wireless device with your Galaxy Tab. You can easily deactivate Bluetooth in the Notifications panel. Follow these directions.

Turn Off Bluetooth

You can turn off Bluetooth in the Settings options under Wireless and Network. Follow these directions to turn off Bluetooth.

1. Tap Apps from any Home screen.

2. Tap the Apps category.

3. Tap Settings.

4. Tap Bluetooth to turn off the setting.

Quick Settings for Bluetooth

The Galaxy Tab 2 offers an even quicker way for you to access the Bluetooth setting by providing quick settings in the notification panel. Simply tap in the far-right corner of the status bar located at the bottom right of your Tab's screen and tap the green Bluetooth setting to turn it off.

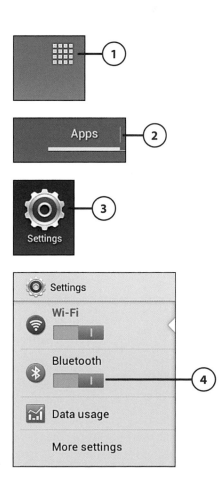

Solving Random Galaxy Tab Issues

The occasional hardware or software glitch happens to even the best of electronic devices. You might encounter an issue, although rare, where an app you are using freezes, a wireless device proves difficult to pair with your Galaxy Tab 2, the touchscreen becomes unresponsive, or landscape orientation is not available at all times. Fortunately, it is not very difficult to troubleshoot some of these issues. If you should happen to come across a problem that you can't solve yourself, there are plenty of channels for you to find technical support.

Difficulty Turning Your Tab On or Off

On rare occasions, you might find your Galaxy Tab 2 stubborn when you try to turn it on or off. It might appear that the device has locked or become unresponsive. If this happens to you, hold the Power button for eight seconds to see if it responds. If this does not work, you might need to let your Tab sit for a few seconds before you again try holding the Power button for eight seconds.

Touchscreen Becomes Unresponsive

This tip assumes that your Galaxy Tab 2 and any app you are using is responsive, but the touchscreen is not responding to your touch. If you attempt to use your Galaxy Tab 2 touchscreen while wearing conventional gloves, it does not work. This can prove inconvenient on a very cold day, so you might want to consider a capacitive stylus for your Galaxy Tab.

Your Tab uses a capacitive touchscreen that holds an electrical charge. When you touch the screen with your bare finger, capacitive stylus, or special static-carrying gloves, it changes the amount of charge at the specific point of contact. In a nutshell, this is how the touchscreen interprets your taps, drags, and pinches.

The touchscreen might also be unresponsive to your touch if you happen to have a thin coat of film on your fingertips. So no sticky fingers, please.

Force Stop an App

Sometimes an app might get an attitude and become unruly. For example, an app might provide a warning screen saying that it is currently busy and is unresponsive, or it might give some other issue warning to convey that a problem exists. If an app is giving you problems, you can manually stop the app. After you stop the app, try launching it again to see if it works correctly. Follow these steps to force stop an unruly app.

Stop a Rogue App

You can stop a problematic app from running by accessing the Manage Applications option located under the settings. You can also report a problem regarding the app to the developer from the same Settings options. Follow these directions.

1. Tap the Apps button on a Home screen.

2. Tap the Apps category.

3. Choose Settings.

4. Tap Application Manager.

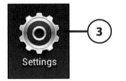

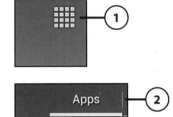

5. Tap Running at the top of the screen to view only the apps that are currently running.
6. Tap the problem app.
7. Tap Stop. The app stops running. Take note that you can tap the Report option to report a problem to the app's developer.

Settings
Show cached processes
Wi-Fi
Bluetooth
Data usage
More settings
Device
Sound
Display
Wallpaper
Power saving
Storage
Battery
Application manager
Personal
Accounts and sync
Location services
Security
Language and input
Back up and reset
Application manager
Downloaded
Running
All
Gallery 24MB
1 process and 0 services
Settings 40MB
1 process and 0 services
Software update 7.5MB
2 processes and 1 service 93:11:47
Factory Test 4.9MB
1 process and 1 service 93:11:54
Google Services 16MB
1 process and 2 services 93:11:45
Software update 2.3MB
1 process and 1 service 18:11
Maps 7.3MB
1 process and 1 service 93:12:00
Game Hub 2.1MB
1 process and 1 service 93:11:12
AccuWeather.com 4.1MB
1 process and 1 service 93:11:33
Media Hub 3.8MB
1 process and 1 service 93:11:32
S Suggest 3.2MB
1 process and 1 service 05:33
Bluetooth share 3.4MB
1 process and 2 services 45:26
Music Player 9.5MB
1 process and 1 service 00:41
Next Issue 5.8MB
AllShare Play 3.4MB
1 process and 1 service 93:11:57
Samsung keyboard 18MB
8:38
5
6

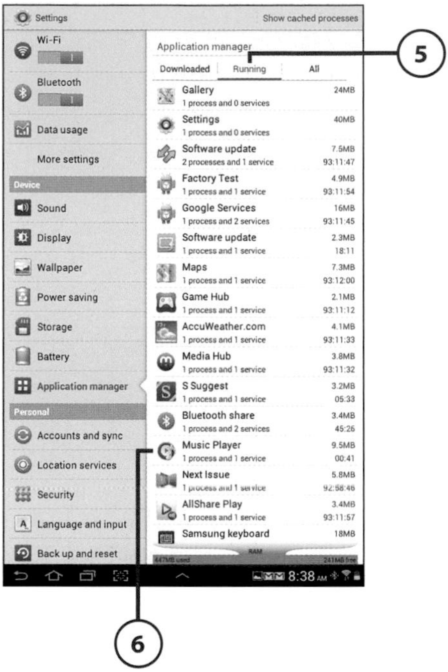

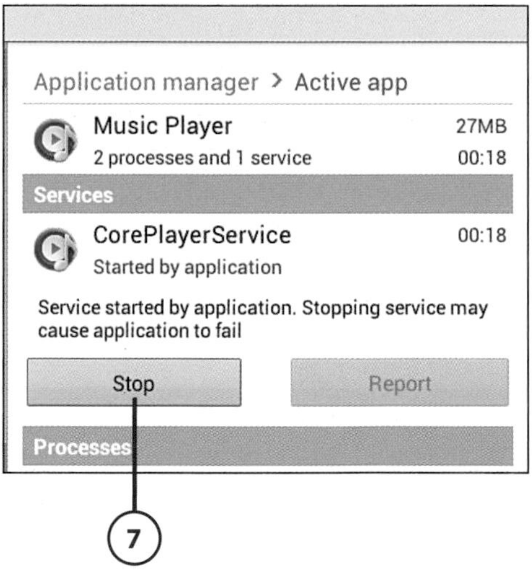

Application manager > Active app
Music Player 27MB
2 processes and 1 service 00:18
Services
CorePlayerService 00:18
Started by application
Service started by application. Stopping service may cause application to fail
Stop
Report
Processes
7

Battery Does Not Charge

If you find that your battery is not charging, first start with the power outlet. Is the outlet supplying power? Is the power strip turned on? Plug something else into the outlet to see if it works, or try another outlet.

Make sure that everything is connected properly. Is the adapter secure on both ends? If the outlet supplies power and the cables are connected properly, but the battery still does not charge, try another cable. If this does not solve the issue, your battery might be defective. Contact Samsung technical support. (See the "Getting Technical Help" section later in this chapter for more information about how to contact Samsung.) There is no way for you to remove the battery yourself.

Overheating

Overheating is rare, but if your Galaxy Tab becomes too hot and regularly turns itself off, you might need to replace the battery. You can tell if your Tab is getting too hot by holding it in your hands. Use caution.

Landscape Orientation Does Not Work

The orientation setting on your Galaxy Tab 2 could be set so that your Tab stays in either portrait or landscape mode, regardless of how you hold the device. If your Tab no longer utilizes landscape orientation, first check the setting for screen orientation. For the 10.1" Tab, you need to go into the settings under Screen and ensure that the Auto-Rotate Screen option is enabled. A green check mark next to this setting means that it is enabled.

Landscape Orientation and Apps

Not every app on the Android Market was developed to take advantage of the landscape orientation of your Galaxy Tab. If you notice this issue while using an app, close the app and then see whether your Tab can situate itself in landscape orientation.

Check the Orientation Lock Button

The Galaxy Tab 2 has an Auto-Rotate setting that must be selected for the screen to adjust from portrait to landscape mode, depending on how you hold the device. You can easily confirm that the Auto-Rotate setting is selected from the Settings menu.

1. Tap Apps on any Home screen.

2. Tap the Apps category.

3. Tap Settings.

4. Tap Display.

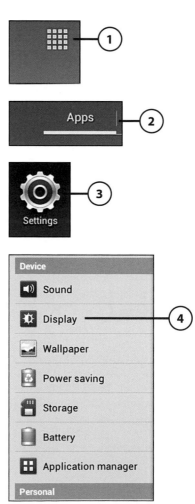

5. Locate the Auto-Rotate Screen setting and confirm that there is a green check mark in the check box. If a green check mark is not present, tap the field to activate the setting. Your Galaxy Tab screen should now adjust to the orientation in which you hold the device.

Display

General

Brightness   ⊙

Screen timeout   ⊙
After 5 minutes of inactivity

Auto-rotate screen   ☑

Font

⑤

Troubleshooting Wi-Fi Accessibility Problems

Your Galaxy Tab 2 provides you the convenience and flexibility of wireless Internet access via Wi-Fi connectivity. Along with this convenience and flexibility comes the potential for connectivity issues regarding wireless networks. If you are unable to access a Wi-Fi network, or if your connection is sporadic, there are some troubleshooting tips you can use to pinpoint basic accessibility options.

Make Sure Wi-Fi Is Activated

First and foremost, make sure that the Wi-Fi antenna is on. You can determine this by looking in the right corner of the system bar at the bottom of your Galaxy Tab screen to see whether the Wi-Fi icon is visible. If it is not on, you can tap in the lower-right portion of the system bar at the bottom of the screen and then tap the Wi-Fi option to activate the setting.

Wi-Fi Antenna

Check Your Range

If Wi-Fi is activated on your Galaxy Tab 2 and you still cannot connect, take note of how far away you are from the Wi-Fi access point. You can be only 115 feet from a Wi-Fi access point before the signal becomes weak or drops altogether. Structures such as walls with lots of electronics can also impede a Wi-Fi signal. Make sure you are close to the access point or turn on the access point's range booster, if it has one, to improve your connection.

Reset Your Router

The issue might not be your distance from the Wi-Fi access point, a signal-impeding barrier, or your Galaxy Tab 2. As a last resort, you might need to reset the router. After you reset your router, you have to set up your network again from the ground up.

Reset the Galaxy Tab 2 Software

If all else fails and your technical problems still persist, as a last ditch effort you might need to reset the Galaxy Tab software. Resetting your Galaxy Tab software restores your Tab to the factory defaults, just like when you took it out of the box for the first time. Consider contacting support before you reset your Tab, but if you must, follow these directions to reset the device.

Reset Your Tab (Galaxy Tab 10.1")

You can reset your tab from the Back Up and Reset options located in the settings. Consider resetting your Tab as a last effort for solving persistent performance issues.

1. Tap the App button from any Home screen.

2. Tap the Apps category.

3. Choose Settings.

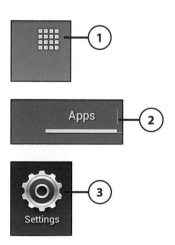

4. Scroll down and tap Back Up and Reset.

5. Choose Factory Data Reset.

6. Tap the Reset Device button.

7. Tap the Delete All button to confirm. Your Tab is returned to its factory state.

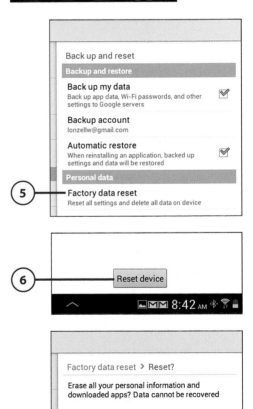

Getting Technical Help

There are many outlets available where you can find help if you run across a Galaxy Tab technical problem that you can't seem to beat. Although limited, the user's manual is a good place to start. You can download the correct manual for your Galaxy Tab model online, in the form of a PDF, and scan the table of contents or perform word searches in the document pertaining to your problem. In most user manual PDFs, topics in the Table of Contents are often linked to the section they pertain to within the document, so when you find what you are looking for, click the topic and jump to the page.

Websites and Galaxy Tab forums are also a great way for you to get support for your device. Type a search phrase, such as "Galaxy Tab Google Calendar sync problem," into Google. Chances are there are plenty of people who are experiencing the same issue. Doing some online research of your own could save you a few minutes on the telephone with technical support and help you solve your problem more quickly.

Contact Your Cellular Provider or Samsung

The Samsung website is a great resource for getting help with technical issues with your Galaxy Tab 2. The Samsung website (http://www.samsung.com/us/support/) offers support via Twitter, Facebook, Google Plus, as well as by phone (1-800-726-7864). Before you call, you need to have your device's model number so that you can give it to the technical support representative.

Locate Tab Model Number

You can find the model number on the box that your Tab shipped in, and you can also find it in the Settings menu. Follow these directions to locate your Galaxy Tab's model number within the Settings menu.

1. Tap the Apps button from any Home screen.

2. Tap the Apps category.

3. Choose Settings.

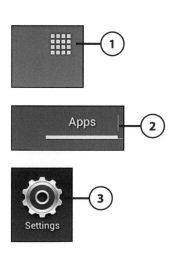

4. Scroll down and tap About Device.

5. Locate your Tab's model number in the About Device field on the right of the screen.

Index

Q-R

S